SHELL SEA SHELL

LIAM LYNCH was born in Dublin in 1937. As a child, he lived in counties Cork and Limerick. After the death of his father (a sergeant in the Gardai Siochana) he returned to Dublin, where apart from stays in Birmingham and London, he has remained since. *Shell, Sea Shell* is Liam Lynch's first published novel. He has already won a reputation as a playwright. His plays include: *Do Thrushes Sing in Birmingham?* (Abbey Theatre, 1963); *Soldier* (Peacock Theatre, 1969); *Strange Dreams Unending* (RTE Radio, 1973); *Krieg* (Project Arts Centre, 1981).

Shell, Sea Shell
On the sea shore
Shall I see my true love
No, never more

Shell, Sea-Shell

LIAM LYNCH

WOLFHOUND PRESS

First published by
WOLFHOUND PRESS
68 Mountjoy Square, Dublin 1

This book is published with the assistance of The Arts Council (An Comhairle Ealaíon) Dublin, Ireland.

British Library Cataloguing in Publication Data
    Liam, Lynch
    Shell, sea shell.
    I. Title
    823'.914[F]   PR6062.Y5/

    ISBN 0-86327-030-1
    ISBN 0-905473-80-9 (cased edition)

Cover illustration Keggy Carew
Typography Michael O'Brien
Typesetting by Print Prep Ireland Ltd.

Printed by Billing & Sons Limited
Worcester

In memory of my father

Part I

ANNA

Someone mentioned the sea.

It was a warm summer's evening. There was an almost overwhelming smell of flowers. Those her mother had scattered all over the flat (even the bathroom) and those which grew in neat, orderly beds in the centre of the square outside, ringing the splattering fountain, the sounds of which were insidious and sometimes wakened her in the early hours of the morning. Their fragrance wafted everywhere about the village and secured tenure of every house flanking the square through the open french windows of the apartment buildings and the windows of the small, neat houses. Altogether, they obliterated the faint smell of the summer food they were eating.

She stopped eating and cocked her head as though having heard a whistle. "What's the sea?" she asked her Uncle Alex who was seated immediately opposite her at the table and who was the only one of her family who could be relied on to answer what the others dismissed as pestering questions.

He laughed his round, jovial laugh which she found so attractive and which so irritated her mother. He wiped his mouth with a white linen napkin in broad, generous strokes. He seemed greatly amused and his small, dark eyes shone in anticipation as he gulped a drink from his clear, stemmed glass and this time dabbed faintly at his mouth with his bunched napkin.

"The sea," he said, "is a vast body of water" — here he paused and raising his arm with some inches of starched cuff showing below the sleeve and held together with links of pure gold in the style of ancient imperial coins he gently raised and dipped his plump, soap-scented hand. "Undulous, gently murmurous and shot through with the silver of sunlight."

"Alex," her mother exclaimed, her voice shrill with, for her, uncharacteristic admiration. "How poetic!" Alex smiled, inclined his head in mock recognition and raised his wineglass in silent toast.

How very beautiful, she thought, thinking of something she had vaguely heard of at school and remembered as being coloured blue on the maps of Europe and The World which hung on the classroom walls, but had never actually seen. Her food lay before her on the plate already abandoned though her knife and fork were still poised above it.

She concentrated. She memorised it. As though it was a prayer to be repeated privately from time to time or on given occasions and always with respect if not indeed, love. 'The sea is a vast body of water, undulous, gently murmurous and shot through with the silver of sunlight.'

It was the last time they were together. She never saw her paternal grandparents again, or her Uncle Alex. All perished in the forward sweep of the German forces through the Low Lands that summer.

Uncle Alex, she heard her mother whisper to someone on the lorry, while under that strange compulsion to talk to total strangers in times of danger, imparting to them confidences which otherwise would not have been shared with anyone, however well they were known — died, when in the faint dawn of the day of invasion he roused himself suddenly from sleep and dressing hurriedly, rushed from the house like a mad dog and circled about on the dew-dampened cobbles of the square like an animal scenting distant but approaching danger. Her mother heard his movements and went to the window of her bedroom and opened it. Everything was still and silent. The lavatory flushed in one of the flats, its sounds carrying embarrassingly far in the quiet morning air. In the centre of the square the flowers were still sleeping, untempted by the first, faint infiltratory lights of dawn, to unfurl. The fountain, ordinarily so thin and feeble, sounded like a cataract.

Suddenly she realised what had so alarmed Alex. Silence. Mere silence. The silence of a dawn unwelded to the dawn chorus. The hair at the nape of her neck, and more curiously, those in her nostrils, bristled in terror. Then they came, slicing and sluicing the brightening air of day. Aircraft. Structurally beautiful as they swept towards the sleeping cities of the west coast. Dawnstruck, they shimmered despite their drab camouflage, creating in the mind and memory a silver dazzle which, like chance sunlight rippling across the body of shallow water, instantly impresses on the mind the image of swift, white movement. A memorable beauty. Incidental to the prime purpose. Which was destruction and death.

Something went wrong.

A craft accidentally unleashed its load of bombs over the sleeping countryside. For the most part, they exploded innocently on open fields. One bomb, however, remained jammed in the bomb bay until the plane was over the village. It fell and exploded in the square. Windows were shattered and long, dagger-like shards of glass blew everywhere. Uncle Alex was struck by such a shard or possibly by some shrapnel. It severed his head in one clean stroke, causing it to go plonk, plonk, plonk, down the gentle, sloping cobbles towards the gutter — or so she heard her mother say — for all the world like a turnip having fallen from the heaped cart of a farmer bringing turnips to town on market day.

"Would you believe that?" her mother asked the totally unheeding stranger, as they plunged westwards on a lorry so packed with humans ready at the slightest provocation to murder still less maul.

"Plonk, plonk, plonk."

"For all the world like a turnip."

"Would you believe that?"

Nobody listened.

Nobody cared.

Why should they?

In the lorry the sense of encroachment as others pressed close violated her body and her sense of being, in a manner she had

never known before. She tried to ignore the whimpering
voice of her mother, the sight of sweat in huge beads like
vulgar pearls, streaking down her face and neck and into the
deep cleft just below the neckline of her dress. Unbelievably
her mother was wearing a fur coat which she had heavily
sprayed with scent from an atomiser before they had taken
flight and bought and fought their way onto the, even then,
crowded lorry. The bowels of the hysterically chattering
woman had, like those of some others on or in the lorry,
loosened in fright. The stench was foul and more demeaning
than an open wound. Like the others, her mother pretended
it was someone else was guilty. But the evidence was there.
In her eyes. As it was in the eyes of others.

Everywhere there was noise. Screaming across the land, the
clogged roads, the open fields. Screeching in the skies above
as fighter plane fought fighter plane until one was struck and
fell to earth with a detonation they no longer heard or cared
about and a burst of flame, they managed to convince them-
selves, could neither sear nor consume. They headed for one
of the smaller ports, farther up the coast, in the hope of
securing passage to England.

Summer was rife in the trees they passed. Lilac clusters
were thick on the high neglected bushes. Which in many
cases were as tall as trees. Higher than the houses themselves.
Ditches were thick with grasses and sedges. Amongst them
clustered the first summer flowers. Tiny pinpoints of white
or blue. Button-sized white and bigger yellows. In the ditches
where they could catch the sunlight. Where there was shade,
growths sprouted, all water bloated. Stalks, lush and green.
Foliage, shiny and spreading. Flowers, largely white and
repugnantly scented. Repellent. Capable of tainting on
touch.

In a few places they passed the bodies of dead animals
where they had fallen. Their bodies already beginning to
swell. She once saw a dead horse in a field outside the town,
its belly swollen almost to bursting point. The teeth bared.
The tongue protruding, thickened and lengthened. Purple
with a light green flush. Like the old velvet curtains on the
parlour windows of the house of a friend of hers. Flies tatted
about the mouth, picking greedily on the scum on the teeth,

the dried silver slime of the tongue.
  Everything registered acutely.
  Nothing aroused emotion.
  Emotion was a hard clod of earth.
  Entangled inextricably
  In her bowels.

The seaport town seemed strangely deserted. People stood in doorways and watched the stream of refugees move down the steep slopes to the harbour like those watching a festival of flowers or a carnival parade which each summer trudged its way along the same route. Year in, year out. Costumes always the same. The band thumping out what to elders were tired old tunes. Only the children watched. With, in some cases, terrible frankness. The girls stood on tippy-toe or with one leg behind the other, their feet entwined. Thumbs in mouth, idly sucking. Eyes bright and registering, round and O. The boys in most cases adopted mannish stances. Hands deep in pockets. Lips trebling soundless tunes between their apple-white teeth rooted in firm, pink gums. Others refrained, almost haughtily, to even stand and stare. They played and skipped about. Their voices shrill with merriment. Or perhaps they were trying to scream down their experiences of the morning. They too watched. And registered what they saw from their eyes slit with cunning. All the better to see. Or simply as a protection against the strong light of the sun towards which their faces turned like sunflowers fated to follow the bright, white centre of day as it crossed the sky.
  There were minute scenes of carnage in the town. Lower down by the port. Some civilians' cars sheltered by the kerbs or lay turned on their sides in the gutter. Burnt out. As though aged and rusted and their material life finished all in a matter of seconds. They stank sweetly for reasons she didn't at first understand. Unconsciously she salivated. Realised why. And looked elsewhere. They passed some military vehicles. Tanks. And armoured cars and lorries. Some were shattered. Some fire-blackened. As neatly crisped as the civilian cars. The bodies of the occupants were hanging out of the tanks. They hung face down. Their upper bodies lax.

Hands hanging down beside them as if reaching for the earth. Their heads were intact. Or half blown away. On the broad tracks of the tanks or the engines of the armoured cars, other bodies slumped. Their faces whole and clean. Their eyes open to the sunlight. Some had frail smiles which seemed to hover about their lips. Surprise at their mortality. Their humanity. In the face of death.

The one total realisation

Of their short lives.

Some lay ignominiously broken backed by the tanks. Others managed to cling on having resisted the impulse to flee and were sprawled about in postures so common on war memorials. There was a terrible poignancy about them. A barbaric sense of loss and waste. In some an attitude of offering. A vast proferrence of the spirit. The fire within. Which men liked to think of as immeasurable when given. Trivial when taken.

Later she was to remember how young they were.

And how denied.

How fair and unfulfilled.

How greedy, war.

How promiscuous.

Elsewhere were visible the bodies of civilians. Unmarked. Stunned or gunned into death. Others were masses of unfamiliar colours. Bright red flesh and curiously coloured entrails. Bright green. Muted purples. And long meshed threads of a spurious too-white white. Spread about as thought they were nothing but bundles from a slaughterhouse improbably wrapped in assorted paper. Frocks. Or suits. All loose. Scattered because the weak brown paper couldn't take the strain.

And burst open.

Some whimpered at the sight.

Some paled and sickened and bowed their heads as if in Some inner humility.

And vomited down their fronts.

Others stared.

And saw nothing.

"I'll forget all this," she said silently.
"Some day."

The sea was filthy. The colours of a fouled gully being washed down outside the cattle market on market day stank. Like a cesspool. It wasn't vast. It was a very finite body of heavy, slurping liquid caught within the embrace of the outstretched arms of the harbour. It neither sang. Nor sighed. It wheezed. Like someone with a chest complaint being strangled to death by the unalterable constriction of the windpipe. It wasn't silvershot. It was shitgreen. Dull, unreflective. On which islands of debris entangled with the knobbed tendrils of seaweed moved slowly, almost imperceptibly. Sewage from a broken pipe poured in and mixed with spreads of oil farther down the quayside. Everything was in a remote way extraordinarily silent though somewhere in the background bedlam rampaged. The sky was free from fighters. Only the gulls screaming and screeching, marshalled themselves in magnificent poises of body — a fixture of wingbones with overlapping layers of feathers, stilled themselves high at their most glorious and then swooped to feast on whatever appealed to their sight.

Or appetite.

Ships were loading. Naval vessels, some flying less familiar flags and other with flags totally unrecognisable. Some were commercial ships. Traders. And tramp steamers. Some were new looking in dark grey or white. Others black grim vessels constructed for nothing but the servitude of coal runs or trading with remote uninteresting places. Ships which may well pass in the night. Unseen. And if seen, unremembered. Everywhere, particularly at the gangways, armed personnel were posted. Some in what were readily recognisable as uniforms. Others, old sweats in dirty oiled trousers and dark blue sweaters were armed and equally vigilant. Boarding proceeded in an orderly way underwritten by a savage desperation which could at any moment erupt into violence. Or collapse in tiny inner despair. Some produced documents which gained them that most desirable of things, a footstep on the gangway. Others, despite pleas in voices which were softly seductive or loudly plaintive, were turned back or more insistently forced to retreat under threat of guns, the holders of which were now more deeply despised than the enemy behind. Most looked stricken. Or numb. Some were so angry they bit their lips and blood streaked down their chins unnoticed. A young woman in summer whites smiled faintly, bowed formally as if denied a favour to which she was entitled by some high personage, suffered a slight rejection and calmly withdrew with the dignity only the rejected beggar can summon. One couple, man and wife, rigidly retreated as if they had suffered some social snub. Slight in itself. But searing, and likely to be remembered all their lives. So much so that the memory might well be the one they most vividly recall as they lay dying.

Fortunes were offered.

People stood and poked about desperately in their wallets or money purses and handbags and held aloft bunched hands sprouting paper money like plants sprouting flowers. They were unfamiliar. Bright black brushed with vermilions, bright violets or muted blues. High value notes which she had never seen before. Like exotics they blossomed in starkly effective colour combinations. There on the quayside. In the warm heat of the summer's day. Elsewhere others held aloft gold coins which caught the sunlight and flashed like the rayed monstrance she had seen carried through the Catholic quarters of the town on a feast-day in high summer. And before which people knelt. And bowed low. And blessed themselves. Here the scarce metal met with no such prostrations or signs of worship. Though they must have represented fortunes to the armed, alert figures on the ships and gangways. The sight evoked no visible response, it might well have aroused some inner greed or hunger. Outwardly in some rare cases it produced pity. More frequently, contempt. One woman abandoned her bag and baggage, including her purse. And bunching up the front of her frock thrust her lower body forward and teeth bared in a snarl of raw sexuality, puckered

the mound beneath as if to induce the secretions necessary
for easy entry.
Like a low whore.
Offering herself
For nothing.
Nobody noticed.
Or if they did,
Cared.
The body, living or dead
Had been devalued.

She stared. And saw. Nothing. Yet everything registered.
With stark, cold clarity. Images. All of which were impressed
on her mind with the precision of an intricate design being
impressed on soft, pliable glass. Still fluid and workable.
"I'll forget all this," she told herself with an inner whimper.
"No, you won't," a voice replied. Her own. The interior
voice. More steeled. Stronger than the other. The voice we
suppress. Because it tells us what we don't want to hear.
The truth.
The bombers came. Followed by the Stukas. They first
sought and caught many of the laden ships which had already
cleared the mouth of the harbour. The others sought as their
targets the packed, reasonably large but yet totally inadequate
vessels about to cast off. And those still loading. Everything
happened at once. Or seemed to. They registered in imagery
which was without sequence or order of any kind. Whatever.
They were like a packet of holiday snapshots or a handful of
seaside postcards. Or views. Which she could later shuffle at
will or lay out for display or examination without any refer-
ence to the sequence in which they were originally shot. Each
was a picture. A story in itself. They were eloquent. Much
too much so. Just beyond the hidden entrance of the harbour,
vessels erupted in an explosion of flame and disintegrating
metal and materials. Tiny figures, hardly recognisable as
human beings, were slung out on all sides. There was some-
thing grotesque, demeaningly amusing in the spray of severed
hands and legs. And heads. Just a momentary demeanment
before they, too, disintegrated. White sprays of water billow-

ed out and up, cupping the scenes of destruction like the outer spread of petals protecting the heart of a flower. White water gave birth to dark, dense smoke. And one was struck by the silence. On the quays people flung themselves on the ground to protect themselves. Bullets spattered about them. They moaned faintly. Or not at all. And died. Just died. Others raised themselves finding it difficult to believe they were still alive. A few raised themselves on one hand like figures stricken on a battlefield confronted by a flow of blood from the mouth or some other wound. Blood. Their blood. Surprised. Very surprised. As if until then they believed they were merely carved wooden figures. Or human-sized dolls stuffed with old shredded rags or packing straw. From behind came the stutter of anti-aircraft, which had no effect.

Whatever.

Stunned silence into which all noise and sound of every kind was sucked or simply absorbed. Then bedlam. There was a noise from the crowds on the quay. Low at first. Like a moan. But rising sharply. Until it became louder. Much louder. Ugly. And distorted. People swept towards the gangways. From higher up in the town came sharp cries. Yelps. Heading down towards the quays was a convoy of trucks. Lorries. Buses. There could be no mistake about their destination. Or what they hoped for. Shots were fired. In the air. The armed men on the gangways and on board ship were now whitefaced. And thin lipped. Their tongues were very moist. They licked their lips frequently and uncertainly. On the very young, those whose chins were covered with a light down, the effect was of improbably applied lipstick. Red. Or poppy. Or red-orange. Their eyes were sleepy. Half open. Like those of some dozing, contented animal. But their bodies were alert. Every muscle taut. Ready to act. Instinctively. To do the right thing. They seemed reluctant to be trapped on the quays and face death. For that fraction of mankind now swarming towards them.

Orders were barked. In several languages. All of which left no doubt that whoever did the barking was also clearly capable of doing the biting. If at all. Necessary. Gangways were retrieved. Some more rapidly than the others. Seeing them slide into the ships some made a dive for them. Gained a footing. But not a hand-hold and slid down into the waters between the ships and the quayside. The ships heaved to and fro gently and most were crushed to death. Instantly. The ship nearest them began to retrieve its gangway. Suddenly her mother dashed forward. Up the gangway. Halfways up she paused. Terror stricken. As though she had forgotten. Someone. Something of great value. Sweating heavily she darted down the gangway. She had been left clutching the battered suitcase on the quay. She experienced fleetingly a sharp sense of utter betrayal. And loss and abandonment. And other complex emotions she couldn't sort out. Not just then. Joy welled inside her like a new spring breaking through the arid crust of the earth for the first time as she saw her mother retrace her footsteps. To fetch her. She expected to be roughly, almost thoughtlessly dragged up the planks to the safety of the deck. Instead her mother's face twisted itself into ugly anger. As if confronting a thief. She bunched her fists and time and time again, she struck. Until she succumbed to the onslaught and fell to the quayside. Her mother grabbed the suitcase and dashed back up the gangplank. She had barely jumped to safety before the gangway was retrieved. She sweated and heaved. Trying to catch her breath after her exertions. Her hair was matted with sweat. It poured down her face and neck. But she looked curiously happy. She hugged the case close to her. And kissed it. Once. Twice. As if it were a child she was caressing. And reassuring. The ship cast off. As did others. Afraid they might become sitting ducks for further bombers or fighters. They headed towards the mouth of the harbour and the narrow channel to safety which lay immediately beyond. They clotted about the narrow mouth. And somehow or other, got through. They passed out of sight. Leaving her.

Or so it seemed.

Even as she stared in stark disbelief at the departing ships. On one of which was her mother. Clutching a heavy suitcase. Caressingly. She heard the sound of running feet. They could have no significance for her. Or so she thought. Even as she thought, they stopped. By her. She was swept up. Unceremoniously. And carried back to and aboard a tramp steamer. She was conscious only of a man's strong arms about her. A draught of bad breath. The sight of decayed teeth. Like rotten posts. Against a bleak, black skyline. She both felt and heard. Or so it seemed to her. The hurried beat of a stout heart set inside a barrel chest. Echoing in a sound chamber. Of sorts. Once safely aboard, he lifted her high. Skywards. Triumphantly. Kindly. "There you are miss," he said. And kissed her lightly. On the right cheek. And then he went away.

She never saw him again.

They left the quay with little ceremony. Behind them, as they headed for the harbour, figures splashed into the water. Like so many swimmers, fully clothed. Having a crazy obstacle race. Fully clothed. In the water. They swam desperately. Against the swell. As everyone watched they became water-logged. They thrashed about. Floundered. Went under and drowned. A few kept swimming. Their efforts above all else. Valiant. Met with no encouragement. Hatred seeped from the sweating bodies of those watching. So strong. So pungent. It might well have been visible as a vapour. To those in the water. One enraged woman leaned over the railing of the stern and spat. With cold, calculated deliberation. She worked the muscles of her throat furiously. Mustering spittle. To hurl down at the now greatly reduced number of swimmers in the water. As if trying to drown them. In spittle. Could she have mustered phlegm, she would have. Perhaps to better effect.

They gained the narrow channel outside the harbour. The swimmers were no longer visible. But the woman at the stern of the ship kept spitting. Everywhere there was wreckage. And the signs of minute carnage they had become so used to. They were packed like cattle on a cattle boat. They excreted freely. Because the lavatories were clogged from so much use on so many mercy runs. Some were faintly sick. Others violently so. But now no one felt demeaned. Or reduced in any way. Whatever. They no longer kept their eyes downcast. In shame. Now they held themselves erect rigidly. Their eyes open like narrow slits. Watching for the slightest sign of contempt. Or what they could interpret as contempt. And gave the impression that if they found what they were looking for they would streak towards the offender and sink their teeth. Into a jugular vein. And sever it. With their teeth. A woman held a screaming infant. In precisely the same way one would hold a bag of potatoes. Indifferently. The child continued to scream. Its mouth sought a breast. As if its life depended on it. As indeed it did. The woman bared part of her upper body . . . absently. As if hearing the child's cries from a great distance. Insistent. And somehow in a vague way, it concerned her. The child clamped its mouth about the nipple of the exposed breast. And sucked and sucked and sucked. Drawing no nourishment whatever. It screamed. Its face red and distorted with rage. And anger. Its mother held it some distance from her. And shook it furiously. Like a child rattled a money box to assess how much money was in the box. The child scream-ed louder than before. And again there emanated from the tightly packed mass on the boat, the same hatred as before. As if people hated with the same glands they perspired with. The woman helplessly clamped the child to her and left it to suck a terror-dried breast.

They landed at one of the mid-eastern English ports. And were welcomed. With steaming mugs of coffee and thick sandwiches of cornbeef. They had red blankets draped about their shoulders as if they were being ennobled in some obscure ritual. A woman. Nunnish. In her mid-thirties or so. Very handsome, if not beautiful in an austere way, walked about. Repelling with a soft smile all efforts to help or even touch her. She held a bruised can of sliced apricots in her hand as though she was a chaste and choice maiden. Very young and fated for the love of a prince. Just having picked the first violets of spring. Marvelling at their scented beauty. Their resilience to the cold of winter. And the fact that so simple an act of gathering them could move her so much. Like some-one in a ballet. Or an opera. Or a story being mimed. She skirted those groups dispensing comforts. Dodged outstretch-ed hands which sought only to succour and console. Then with infinite care she laid her can of fruit on the quayside. And with all the simplicity of a nun, she reached under her

skirt and slipping down her underwear, squatted. And soiled.
And then, as primly as she had taken them down, she pulled
them up. And reaching for her can. Of apricots. Walked
about as before. Shocked. Ice cold. Her actions aroused sheer
disbelief in most cases. Slight disapproval on the part of the
others. None of whom had yet learned the lesson. That
mankind under stress does not disintegrate. It only re-
gresses.

"I'll forget all this," she said.
    "No, you won't," replied the other, inner voice.
    Steeled. Stronger than the other.
    The voice that tells us what we don't want to know.
    The truth.

She found herself
    A limbodic being.
    In a grey, limbo world.
    Only it wasn't. Really grey. It was mostly red. The red
of brick buildings built in the last years of the last century
by various university charities. Those whose charitable monies
built them would have refused to use the largest room as a
box-room and would, most likely, have thought of themselves
as being guilty of inhumane treatment of their horses if they
kept them in such cramped, badly lit conditions. Elsewhere
were rackety warehouses of all kinds. Some glass-roofed, the
bottom of the high walls tufted with persistent, tenacious
grass or dandelions or other pernicious weeds. Behind, not
very far away, lay the docks and the incessant sound of men
at work. With metal. Servicing and repairing ships. Or loading
or unloading. Ships which came bearing cargoes from the
four corners of the earth.
    She was boarded with an elderly couple. As a displaced
person. And an alien. With a tailor, Solly, and his wife. The
woman was grey. Grey featured. Grey eyes and grey hair.
And grey, unhealthy skin. She rarely smiled. If at all. As
though she had sinned. Gravely. Sometime in the remote
past. The very, very remote past. And was now suitably

penitent. Or her heart was so pierced by suffering she could never hope to know. Surcease. Of any kind. For the first time in her life she was poorly clad and shod. In clothing given to her by some obscure Jewish charity. Old shrunken woollens which the grey woman patiently repaired with neat patches of material in blatantly clashing colours. The patching and repairing was perfectly executed by someone who enjoyed grimly such grim servitude. She should have been grateful. But she wasn't. Not at all. The clothes seemed to burn her flesh and caused her intense psychic pain of a kind she never knew existed. Pain she would have thought no human being would ever be called upon to suffer. She was shod with stout boots which had steel studs fitted to their soles and heels. Boots. She considered more fitting a farmhand or some other woker of low estate.

She went to a redbricked school and sat with other children dressed like herself. The standard of cleanliness wasn't uniform. There were children who had slight deformities from the lack of proper food. Some had ringworm and various contagious illnesses generally associated with poverty. Some. A great many were infested with lice. Often she itched with lice she picked up from them. In the afternoon after school the heart-hurt woman would call her aside and lay a sheet of newspaper on the table. Her head was held over the table and the old grey-haired woman raked her hair with a fine comb. The lice fell noisily on the paper. Some were heavy. Big. Blood-bloated. Others, tiny. Just-hatched things. Patiently the woman squashed them. One by one. No matter how thickly they fell or how big or small they were, she squashed them with the thumbnail of her right hand. Leaving them mere bloody smears. The exercise was a daily one. To her, a ritual debasement. To the grey-haired woman, she sensed a curious pleasure. To be prolonged. As long as possible. After each session her scalp was rubbed with a foul-smelling lotion which made her scalp tingle as though she were host to millions of lice. Every Saturday night her hair was washed. And trimmed and its ends scorched by being held over the flickering flame of a candle. On a Sunday she wore bright red ribbons in her hair. Sometimes a white ribbon. Less frequently, a yellow one. She walked with Solly and the heart-hurt woman to the nearest park which was some considerable distance from them. People sometimes complimented her on her hair or admired it aloud when passing. The woman smiled a sickly, subservient smile, the complacent smile of the keeper of the flame. On those walks Solly wore a heavy serge suit which fitted him uncomfortably. She thought he would be better in a suit made of timber planks cut to size and nailed together. The woman wore a blue serge costume with elegant grey braid which was looped attractively along the edges of the severely cut coat and skirt. On her head she wore a ridiculously high hat. Made of straw with a broad ribbon around its band. Onto which was tacked a bunch of cloth violets. The petals of which had all furled as if scorched by frost. Through the green stalks, showed the gleam of dull metal.

They moved stiltedly, jarringly, joggingly over what seemed to her, a joyless, arid waste, their shadows following them as attached areas of black, oddly shaped and unaccountably attached to them. They passed some other children at play, ragged and wild but capable of communing perfectly with the natural world around them. Their feet, they never doubted, were firmly, unshakeably fixed to the earth as they reached skywards in straight, steady growth. She moved jaggedly, lacking their sense of rootage, their uprightness. Her shoulders drooped and even inwardly she crumbled, hearing the sharp, incisive laughter riddled with joy of the other children. Their movement struck her as visually beautiful, their voices silver-toned like the sound of tinkling instruments. The force of life itself flowed generously through their bloodstream as it did in the sap of trees and bushes and of every growing thing. Her blood, it seemed, had dried like dust and blew hollowly through her veins, like rust blowing through a complicated system of minute conduits.

Her dreams were stark and frightening. Sometimes they appeared to have a reality more real than reality itself and were altogether compelling. She dreamed repeatedly. The one dream. Of moving through a decaying mansion of many rooms with bare, much trodden boards in which knots stood in isolation like so many islands which had dared resist the process of decay, which was everywhere about her. The

skirting boards were riddled with holes, the work of rats with
patient, gnawing teeth. She never saw the vermin, the mere
thought of them aroused a strong revulsion in her. But she
could hear the furtive scratching of their claws, the sharp
click of their teeth which aroused a dread of being gnawed
to death by rats with bloated bellies and pink, baby pink
snouts and teeth as sharp and as shredding as serrated steel.
The dread haunted her in her dreams as she progressed from
room to room with walls, the plaster of which was pitted
leprously and painted slime green. On and on she went in the
expectation of what she never quite knew, from one room to
another. Each room alike and each with a door in the far
wall which opened and passed through only to find herself
confronted by a similar room again. To her right and behind
her was the source of a dreadful light, eerie and unpleasant,
in which her form cast no shadow on the floorboards before
her.

The dream drained her
Emotionally and physically,
And somehow left her innately
Diminished in her
Inner self.

Once, as night fled in the first pre-dawn light which sought
supremacy in the still, dark room, she saw the figure of her
mother . . .

Dead. And dressed in a white flowing robe with a short,
white cape draped about her shoulders. In her arm she
cradled flowers.

White arum lilies. Trumpet-shaped with an erect, pollen-
laden stamens. Set cupcentre. Like the ones which grew in
Müllers' garden. Down to the left of the discreetly elegant
house which she was never allowed to enter. At the end of
the pebbled path which skirted the green, clipped lawn
which seemed to remain green when grass elsewhere — in the
park, or fields, curled. And browned. And blackened. In the
intense heat of summer. The path. Pebbled. Which crunched
beneath her feet and led to a pond. Into which water trickled
from the minute penis of a bronze cherub with outstretched

wings. Into the dark waters. Blackly velvet in the shade of the nearby tall pine trees. Water lilies slumbered on in the sensuous mixture of half-light. Half-darkness. Beautiful insularities of cream-white petals touched sparingly with pink. Bobbing gently. On the ever-disturbed surface of the pool, while, below, fat goldfish slipped and slithered languidly, their bodies curving and curling about the stems of the aquatic flowers and plants. Their gills, plainly visible, flickering like eyelashes. There. In the deep. And to the right of the pond. In the shade of the trees. Where least expected. The lilies. Bee-infested. Their sickly, sweet scent seeming to hover about the richly dunged bed. Like a visible vapour. Her mother. With lilies.

Like the statue of a saint. In the cool side aisle of the Catholic church into which she sometimes guiltily trespassed. Relishing the imputed presence of God. In the dim, deserted church, pungent with polished wood and incense lingering on high up in the dark stained rafters. Smelling like the fast-fading flowers in their brass, bright vases. Made more sharply pungent by the day's heat. In darkened spaces. A glorious spread of colours. Like tributary flowers of Ganges colours, cast in mourning on dark, muddied waters. And motes of dust. Moving endlessly in the shaft of light streaming through the stained-glass windows and projecting the colours onto the floor. Moving endlessly in almost clearly defined, sharply confined patterns of light. As if in obedience.

To some august

Law of physics.

Relishing the many sensations of the deep, dusky interior of the church with its flickering sanctuary lamp before the high altar which invoked in her unconscious worship, and the presence in a side aisle of the statue of a saint. Which reminded her of her mother . . .

Dead. Eyes, the pupils of which if caught in a certain light at the correct angle, shone clearly violet. Strikingly so. Regretful if anything. Not grief stricken. Pained. Mildly pained. As if having sought fidelity from the unfaithful. Trust from the untrustworthy. And hope from the hopeless. Knowing. All the time. It would not be so. On the right-hand side of the cape about her shoulders a large red badge. Visible but

not clearly, not in detail. Ruffled about the edges with white
and purple and green ribbons. Like a rosette. Sensing. Know-
ing it had painted or impressed on it. The image of the tuber-
cular Nazarene. Semitic eyes narrowed against the harsh light
of a country with the climatic conditions of a desert. Shot
through with sorrow. Profound pity. Blood. Red blood.
Bursting in bubbles from wounds inflicted by a crown of
entwined thorns. Parched, broken lips, parted like a flower
about to unfold and bring forth promise. Of hopes to come.
Redemption. Through suffering. Death and resurrection.

But hope for whom
She wondered.
The living or
The dead.
She didn't know.
Nor could she.

Her mother's hair. Blue-black. Brushed with green. The green
of mouldering bread. Shining draped in all its black splendour
about her head and shoulders. The white, waxen spaces of
her face and hands and what could be seen of her arms. Her
bare feet. Pitted. With grave sores. Tiny pinpoints. Putrid
craters. Their sides streaked with greens and greys and black.
Rawly red. The minute flowerlike growths which spring from
dead flesh. Signalling the ultimate decay. The ordained
descent into putridity. And its residue. White, fleshless bones,
their unfulfillable dreams and ambitions, unfulfilled. Lapsing
lastly into dust perpetual.

The Adamite destiny
Of all living
Things.

Seeing or half-seeing her mother. Like that. Whimpering. Like a
suckling mammalian deprived of much-needed sustenance and
having to feed on the body's own meagre resources. A sense
of upsurgence between her thighs. Release. Issue. Welcome
warmth and relief. And then the sudden realisation she was
wetting herself. Repugnance and fear. The foul smothering

smells of the tenement rising about her. An admixture of the
excrement which clogged the two lavatories on the landing
below. Or lay, darkly coiled in the dark, dank passages of the
building. And the stale urine which clearly disfigured the
peeling walls and their pocked plaster. And sour soups and
stockpots simmering on the gas and sweat and blood and
other bodily excretions of which she knew nothing.

And which revolted her

Beyond belief.

Solly in the room next door. Coughing and wheezing and
fighting for the first breath of the day which might, one
would have thought, be expected to last the entire day ahead
of him. Beating himself. On the chest. As if he was a sinner.
Acknowledging his transgressions. And pledging penance and
future reform. And retribution. While all the time the elon-
gated fingers of his right hand, with their unusually long
fingernails, each tipped with a scimitar of blue-black dirt, idly
scratched his wrinkled scrotum. And pendant penis. Devoid
of all colour. And strength and assertion. Capable now only
of its secondary function. The drainage of his body's pro-
cessed liquids.

His shrunken manhood. Ransacked by age. Desire. Made
derelict. Ruinous. Without weeds. Coughing. Hoarsely,
mustering the filthy slime which gathered on his chest over-
night. Spitting it now into the tinted jamjar which he kept
positioned under the bed close to hand for such use.

The woman stirred. And so fond of sleep and its oblivion,
she would have slipped into eternal sleep without protest or
complaint. Muttering. Incoherently. Her body coiled in the
foetal position. While dreaming she heard the early morning
sounds of her childhood years in remote Moldavia. Reluctant
now to wake, and admit, those years . . . her life, was gone.
Leaving her a husk. A being with a burnt-out interior. Her
head of sparse, grey hair sporting a mock-crown of green,
entwining foliage and white trumpet flowers, already seeding.

Futility.

Its flowers

And its fruits.

Slipping her body over the side of the bed and baring her body in its entirety and squatting over the pot and pissing steadily, the first spurts dinning noisily against the sides of the enamelled pot. Pissing. Slowly, calculatedly. A simple bodily necessity which unaccountably afforded her an almost primeval pleasure. Finishing. Stumbling half asleep to the rickety table with its tin basin and earthenware jug of cold water. Pouring. The water into the basin. Wetting a cloth and washing herself all over. Totally devoid of modesty. Accepting with the calm clarity of those who have despaired beyond any hope of hope, her reflection in the pocked mirror hanging from a nail on the wall. Before her. Shrunken breasts like the dugs of an old cow. Taunting echoes of her once powerful urge to have them swell. Fruit with rich, thick milk. And have them sucked by the firm, paining gums of a child. Her brief fulfilment. Its annihilation as she cradled the dark, repellent body of her dead girl child. And experienced the steel of pain which penetrated her innermost being. Echoes. But only echoes. No longer crippling in the grief they once aroused, the loss, the longing . . . . Triumph. Of a kind. At having survived. If what she was could be termed survival. Drying her upper body with the coarse, grey towel and then absently cleansing as she had all her life, the shrunken mound between her thighs. Recoiling slightly at the further loss of pubic hair as she saw the thin, broken strands on the cloth. Finishing. Dressing and calling her.

While she trembled in terror and waited for the crash of the door being thrown open. And the harsh merciless voice of the weak for once in a position of strength. Demanding that she come forth. Tearing the bedclothes off her, exposing her humiliated body and the small, ugly, bunched fist raining blows on her face and then cunningly on her upper body while she tried to protect her head with her arms and hands. Her thighs chafed and paining.

Brushed humiliatingly by the woman — with no effort on her part to spare her pain — with a foul-smelling, mustard-coloured lotion. Which smelt of sulphur or decaying vegetation. And which smarted painfully when she tried to walk

and talk with her limited vocabulary about the inconsequen-
tial things children talk about. The other children who
knew nothing about the humiliation of her mind and flesh.
Which after all they couldn't see or even imagine and who
could only wonder why she avoided them. Her voice tinged
with defeat. Her head hanging heavily with misery as though
She was a leper.
Repellently leprous
Or was visibly cancerous
With spreading craters
Of flesh devouring flesh
Openly
And with ignominy.

Sullen silence. The cold, grease-encrusted food which was her
dinner kept for her after school. The room hot and oppres-
sive. Windows tightly shut. Their panes hawed over in a fine,
grey mist. Water bubbling, dribbling down to the window sill
and puddling there. The pot of boiling sheets bubbling on the
stove. Smelling strongly of urine. Her urine.
The woman stirring the sheets with a large wooden paddle.
Glaring at her with bared teeth.
Hating
And yet perversely pleased that she is at least capable
Of that most ineradicable of emotions.
Hatred.
Of herself
And all others.

Somewhere in the dim recesses of the building Solly sang,
drunkenly, a song of racial hurt and ignominy, of the terror
the Cross evoked in his people and how like unhealthy
growths they were permitted to survive only in its shadow
and always under its threat. The song was a raving plea with-
out clemency of any kind, to the God of Israel calling on
Him to smite with His mighty fist the Christian overlords of
his native land, the worshippers of a ranting Semite who
once, in desert-induced delerium, claimed that he was

The Chosen One.
And was most suitably punished
By crucifixion on a
Geophysical prominence outside
The City —
The hill they call
Golgotha.

Trains shunted in the distance.

Aircraft revved their engines to a high whining pitch which had hurt at first. Now they were an acceptably commonplace thing. Their flight no longer interested her. Like a drab bird they flew high into the sky where, against a bright blue backdrop punctured by bloated barrage balloons, they attacked the encroaching enemy aircraft. Aircraft like those which had wreaked such havoc on her home town . . .

That morning. So long ago she couldn't correctly remember when . . . and Uncle Alex had been killed outright by a shard of glass, or was it shrapnel? She couldn't remember. Not quite . . . . So long ago her small blue bedroom with its jolly gollywogs and dancing sailors and milkmaids in prim wide-skirted frocks carried milk in buckets which hung from either side of a length of timber carved in the centre to fit snugly about their necks. Elfin figures played on the blades of grass or swung from the petals of flowers. And the blank areas in between, which with imagination took on a discernible shape of their own. And she tried to will them into life. All those crazy figures of the wallpaper of her room. The people she called her night people all of whom danced in the wavering light of a night light in a blue cut glass holder and shade . . . . Blue, bulbously beautiful and ever comforting . . . . Outside the water fell tricklingly . . . musically, sweetly and as she had so often seen in moonlight, silver.

Aircraft like those caught in a dogfight above her head. Both like big mechanical toys controlled by some masterminds a great distance away and sent screaming into battle like someone moving the figures on a chessboard or counters in a game involving counters . . . . Aircraft like those on that morning so long ago when her mother had grabbed her fur coat into which she had sewn on the advice of Uncle Alex . . . and here her mother would touch her nose as she did whenever describing any of Uncle Alex's transactions which she enviously throught brilliant. . . small diamonds and small pieces of jewellery discreetly bought and hoarded 'in case it should happen' as indeed it did happen and Uncle Alex died, his head severed from his body and which had gone plonk, plonk, plonk, for all the world like a turnip . . . . Just like that.

Heat seemed to rise in visible waves before her and everything about her shimmered and shook and took on a new dimension of active existence which she had never quite noticed before. Floppy headed poppies hung like suspended blood from the grey-haired stems of strong stalks. The stalks were lush and green and quite as tall as she. And the scarlet was very, very scarlet. Here and there yellow ragwort and white flowers which smelt unpleasantly and when touched deposited a foul slime-like substance, faintly green, on the fingers. There were some orange poppies less opulent and striking than the scarlet ones. And two. . . just two. Very, very pale blue poppies of a kind she never knew existed. Close to the gritted ground with its layers of coal dust and powdered cinders, grew white, button-sized flowers. Painfully small, they were painful to stare at for too long. Telegraph poles rose straight and rigid and reached skywards. They didn't run in one straight line as one would imagine they would but in a strangely erratic pattern she couldn't understand. Unlike those she had previously seen, no wires ran from one to the other and on and on from pole to pole into the far distances, to that place in perspective where everything converged at a point the size of a pin and beyond which nothing but nothingness existed. Some of the poles had strong rusted wires holding them in position. Up them crept green foliage sprouting white trumpet-shaped flowers, and which struck her as greedy and grabby in an infinitely patient sort of way.

His shadow cut across hers before she ever realised he was there. She turned in alarm and saw him. His mouth was cleft in a wide, affectionate grin. His eyes shone darkly but attractively so. His hair was jet black and curled and loose about his head and inexplicably she longed to touch and toss it and realised that it was aeons ago since she last touched someone in affection. His white shirt was soiled and open down to the broad belt with its brass buckle at his waist, showing clearly his deeply tanned upper body rivering streams of silver sweat. He radiated warmth and affection and smelt curiously like stagnant water left too long in a vase of flowers . . . foully, yet to her, attractively so.

She saw his thighs, full and muscular, and at the crotch the slight bulge which she stared at having only recently seen the genitals of a male when she came across some men swimming naked in the muddy waters of the river outside their factory. He saw her eyes and noticed where they lingered and smiled in affection and good humour. He stroked her neck and his hard-skinned hand lay gently on her. It was astonishingly warm and, in a way, tender. And so very affectionate and free of the brutality coiled to strike in the bony fists of the sad-faced woman who looked after her and struck her so frequently for reasons she couldn't know. He touched her lightly on the thighs and fleetingly on the slight mound between . . . . And she loved him.

He pressed a penny into her hand. Its size and weight identified it instantly. She knew the wealth it represented but what struck her more was that it seemed infused with the warmth of his warm hand which he slipped inside the open neck of her frock and moved about exploring the geography of her upper body which under the touch of his warm flesh seemed to spring to life for the first time. He took the penny from her and slipped in into his left-hand pocket. "Find it," he murmured softly and gently and slyly guided her hand into the slit in his trousers. Her hand could not penetrate deeply and he held her by the wrist and by shifting the weight of his body, he guided her hand farther in and deeper down and she realised there was a gaping hole in the pocket and her hand went through and she experienced the sweet sensation of touching soft hair between his thighs which seemed as lush and as warm as that on his head. Its softness and warmth surprised and pleased her. He shifted her hand until it rested firmly but gently against his genitals.

He drew her close and kissed her. A moist, sweet kiss. His breath was warm and tasted sweetly. She drew greedily on his lips and pressed hard against his thighs. They parted under her pressure and then he clamped them tightly about her. His eyes shone with endearment. He called her soft, loving names she had never consciously heard before. They had a cradle warmth about them, a familiarity of love she had once known so many years ago she couldn't quite remember when . . . .

A plane exploded in the sky above and fell to earth.

One mechanical toy had destroyed another.

It was peripheral to her vision and consciousness.

Inconsequential when measured against the rough, warm hand exploring between her thighs. He held her tighter and a finger penetrated her orifice. It hurt happily. Her lips parted to receive his tongue and lovingly and longingly he explored the full extent of her mouth. Under pressure from her hands his desire increased and was physically manifest and she experienced a hunger she never knew existed. He arose abruptly and took her roughly by the hand and half dragged, half ran her towards a nearby hut covered in tarred material. It shimmered in the heat and about it grew a profusion of wild flowers and virile thistles. Time was suspended. The moment was made in a sense deeply compelling and temporarily eternal. The pressure of his hand, still warm and not without affection, was now clasped painfully tight about hers. There was more than urgency about it. It was a command of the blood. Uncompromising, demanding of fulfilment. Satisfaction alone could appease it somewhat.

The hut shimmered. Every upright thistle and spread of dogweed seemed heavy with vows of silence, rigid in their silent witness of the scene. He booted in the door and at a glance he took in the contents of the interior. A rusted clothes-wringer, its wooden rolls intact, bleached white from use and outdoor exposure to the elements. Its elaborate cast-iron framework was corroding. Rust red was plainly visible and strangely orange and faint tints of green. Some shovels in a corner, a heap of coal-black sacks and then in another corner a pile of clean sacks neatly folded as if by someone conscientiously preparing for work the following morning and sadly failing to return ever to do so. Poignantly they remained where last she imagined he had carefully laid them.

He shook out the sacks. Dust and a faint gritty residue mingled to provide a cloud of particles. They caught in her throat. She coughed and closed her eyes because it stung to keep them open. With ever increasing urgency he spread the bags and waved aside the dust which seemed touched with gold in the sunlight streaming through the dirty windows, or at least he vainly tried to do so. The sacking spread to his satisfaction. He licked his lips nervously and rubbed his thighs and went outside and almost immediately returned, water dripping from his cupped hands. "Drink," he said shortly. She sipped it, tepid, it lacked both body and vitality, yet it wasn't unpleasant or repugnant. It cleared her throat wonderfully. He bent and untied the laces of his boots and slipped them off. His socks were crudely repaired. They were unclean and smelt strongly of foot odour and a mixture of leather and hot rubber. There was a primitive appeal about the smell which seconds before had so revolted her, she had to catch her breath. Now she extended the nostrils of her nose and wilfully inhaled the gritty air, the oppressive heat of the hut's interior, the one repelling odour and the faint smell of apples she had tasted on his lips when they first had kissed.

He rapidly undressed and kicked aside his clothing. She was forcefully, happily struck by the apparent incongruity of the half-bronzed, half-white body which despite the disparate colouring had a striking unity about it. He possessed, undoubtedly, grace and physical beauty. Fully erect, richly engorged and the deepest of deep purple, his phallus stood erect between his thighs in both pride and command. . . . A command which was a demand and yet there was a supplication in his eyes. He grasped her in warm embrace. Swiftly he stripped her bare and pressed her small body to the warm fullness of his. He drew her down on the sacking with him and slipped his body under hers. Between them was the penis, marvellously strong, yet pliant. Its concentration of heat was astonishing and she felt her entrails and the lower inner organs of her body of which she knew nothing, stir as if from a heavy slumber and assert a terrible hunger. A hunger surpassed temporarily only by that of the mouth. He enfolded her mouth with his and she felt the full extent of his lips, warm, succulent, seeking. With a sweetly tasting tongue he transferred warm spittle to her mouth which she relished before swallowing. His hands were stroking her buttocks and the back of her thighs and she felt warm and liquid and freely capable of light, easy movement, like the children she noticed each time she walked with Solly and the woman in the park.

He swung her lightly aside with an upward movement of his arms. She felt again that pleasant sensation in her stomach which she remembered when as a much younger child and her father was alive, he tossed her skywards and she squealed in delight, a compound of both fear and trust which was to some extent an act of the will — faith of a kind — that her father wouldn't allow her to fall and go crashing to the ground. He sat her lightly on the boards. In a rapid coiling movement he drew his legs behind him and leaning back rested on them. His thighs swelled to their fullest and his phallus was sharply erect like an exotic plant in its flowering season. He drew her gently towards him and downwards in a succession of easy movements, and eased its tip into her mouth. She felt it, its rich, warm springliness, and her mouth clamped about it. She sucked hungrily with all the wild hunger of an infant seeking the milk-yielding nipple. He thrust gently with his thighs, creating the slightest of ripples as though threatening to withdraw what was now to her a vital, warm necessity. A hand cupped her head from behind counteracting any backward movement of her head. Each thrust was sharper now, more urgent than before. The pressure at the back of her head became harder, allowing her to yield less. Her breathing became difficult, her passion increasing in intensity and urgency. His body gave one strong forward thrust. The hand at the back of her head pressed forward. His body tensed to the utmost, like a bow fully taut. It lingered so for one long second and then in a series of spasms his member yielded its fluid which was warm and rich and very pleasurable and trickled down her throat to where the inner organs of the body thirsted frantically for its enrichment. Like rain on barren clay it seeped through almost audibly. The body fed and the inner hunger was satisfied.

He lay back breathing heavily, then freed her legs. He held her and tossed her hair in delight. He kissed her reassuringly and there was intimacy and conspiracy in the kiss. He held her tightly and cradling her as he would a child, turned her aside and enfolding her with his body, he slept. Again she was struck by the innocence of his form, the affectionate warmth of his breath on the nape of her neck. Like someone once flesh and made stone, she was fleshed again — ripe, warm blood coursed her veins. Her flesh was warm and responsive. Her hands regained their sense of the tactile and she drifted into a sleep as secure and as welcome as the sleep she knew grey centuries ago . . . before that day the aircraft had come and they had fled and her mother had deserted her and had been blown to bits on a tramp streamer and with her jewellery and canned meat and fruit, mostly peaches because her mother had an obsessive love of them. That day so long ago she couldn't exactly recall when . . . .

She awoke and was lying flat on the sacking. He was straddling her preparatory to entry, his arched arms and feet taking the greater weight of his big body. "Don't cry," he whispered in a voice almost salted with tears. There was a wounding pity in his eyes, a shame, a sense of hurt. His voice trembled as did his body. She thought of the flop-headed poppies, the scarlet ones, so blood red, which seemed sacramentally wounded. He bared his teeth and tensed his body. "It will hurt," he said, "but don't cry out. Please don't cry out." The supplication of his voice, the very naked appeal of his eyes which so denied his happy, confident self, moved her deeply.

She nodded assent.

He began to penetrate and then began the searing, wounding pain. She bled. He panted. And drove relentlessly forward and upward with each movement. She winced and whimpered softly and she could see pity rent his face followed instantly by undeniable lust. She realised with ice-cold clarity that he could kill her in the very act of entry itself or afterwards, when he had done. Now he sweated freely. Every pore of his body opened and exuded oily secretations which were much more than mere sweat. There was the taste and smell of something animal-like about them. His body glistened with sweat which poured down his dusty body, snake-like, and even in the dim interior of the hut, silvery. It cut a meandering pattern on his skin like a river on its way through arid desert and then branching out to form a rich delta. He reached his climax and his warmth shuddered inside her and spurted deeply within. He sagged, spent, and laughed boyishly and turned over on his massive back, his chest heaving like the flank of a splendid steed. About them dust and grit rose. Caught in the fading sunlight they had all the colours of the prism. A distorted, ever-moving cloud of rainbow colours intermingling freely with the pale delight of both gold and silver. Suddenly he uttered a low moan like an animal in pain, deep, psychic pain. He muttered a prayer which was part oath, part prayer, and wept brokenly and bitterly. He folded in on himself as if by doing so he could contain the grief and pain and remorse which now racked him convulsively.

She bled but not excessively and without much pain. She rested shortly and rose calmly to her feet and swept back her short, straggling hair into its proper position. She adjusted her clothing and smoothed down her dress. She moved slowly, with some pain. She cautiously opened the door of the hut. Low on the skyline the sun, a perfect orb and looking larger than usual, was suspended over the horizon of tatty tenements and warehouses. Without rays and seeming a spent body, it was pink against a pink sky, remarkably so.

She splashed water into one cupped hand from a rain barrel and carefully retraced her steps to where the man sat, coiled in upon himself moaning like someone in extremity. She touched him lightly on the head. He looked at her. Fear, suspicion and, she thought, murder, all showed fleetingly on his face. Then he reached for his vest and dried his face. She wet a finger and drew it across his lips. He licked and inclining his head slightly he lapped the infinitesimal amount which lay in her left hand. She was about to go and get some more water when he caught her roughly and fiercely embraced her and again wept brokenly. She stroked his head and felt the springy liveliness of his mass of black hair. In the weak, waning light which filtered through the dusty window panes of the one small window of the hut his hair shone partly green, partly blue. Enveloped by his warm body she wished she could remain so for ever.

He broke from her and quickly dressed himself, telling her not to move. She lay still on the fragrant sacking stained darkly with her own blood and felt content. He went outside and returned with a jamjar full of water. The jar was clean and the water in it crystal clear. He took off his shirt and with his teeth managed to tear it slightly. Grasping it firmly between both hands he tore a strip off with ease. Tenderly he attended to her thighs with the dampened piece of shirt. He was solemn and concerned and she loved the solemnity with which he attended to her and which seemed close to adoration of a kind.

"It will hurt," he said roughly, trying to hide the soft undertones of tenderness which so belied his physical build and sexual potency. "But not for long." He finished and carefully stuffed the blood-stained piece of shirting into his pocket. He frowned, looking around for further possible incriminating evidence. He could see none and yet he persisted in frowning. Then his eyes lit on the stained sacking. Quickly he tore off the blood-stained piece and folded it neatly, shoved it inside his shirt. He ran his hands through his hair and then wiped his hands on his thighs. He spoke thickly. "I'll go first." He seemed to want something further but changed his mind and before she quite realised it, he was gone. She rose and went to the window and cleared a patch of glass. She saw him move over the small heaps of rubble and profusion of weeds and thistles. There was a marked uncertainty about his movements, a total lack of grace which by its absence wounded her in her love of him. He was, she realised, a fugitive from himself and would never escape and know peace. He never looked back and turning sharply by the railway arch, he passed under and was lost to sight.

She waited and later walking towards the arch she picked

some poppies. The blues she left. The brilliant scarlets and the lesser oranges she gathered into one immense bunch. The greater part of which the old unsmiling woman threw away in exasperation, allowing her to keep the others. She carefully trimmed the stalks and put them in a jam-jar and placed them on the window sill in her bed-room.

She slept dreamlessly until towards morning her mouth hungered for his flesh. She called his name with a mixture of rampant lust and heart-rending pity. The lust of a female body having known the penetration of the male organ. Its paining and pleasurable thrust. . . the climax of the body stretched taut above her for the final assault. . . the burst of fluid, the tidal flow into the innermost reaches of her body. The fleshing of a body she had felt to be of timber or stone. Dead. Unresponsive . . . now warm and fleshed and living.

In one wild afternoon of abandoned fuckeries,

Rebirth.

Resurrection. Of

A kind.

He passed by and she smiled at him now knowing intimately just how every sinewy muscle rippled under his coarse working clothes. He laughed and greeted her affectionately and tossed her hair. Once he pressed a penny into her hand. She bought sugar — the residue of sugar-coated sweets which accumulated in the bottom of the sweet jars in the corner shop. A man with a deep yellow pallor and radiant blue eyes served her with the studied solemnity of one who knows his illness is fatal. He generously scooped out the sugar . . . a wasp trapped in the window buzzed. The man glanced at it companionably. He appeared to have no temp-tation to whack it with a folded newspaper and kill it and sling it out into the street in disgust . . . a foul and fouling insect. He stared at it with his big shining blue eyes . . . eyes of the bluest blue she had ever seen, quite without disgust or hostility of any kind. He filled a paper cone made from a rectangle of newspaper a few days old, a neat bundle of which, carefully cut, lay on the counter before him. The piece he folded for her cone had on it the picture of a man white headed and rabbit featured and smiling the guarded smile peculiar to people with bad or irregular teeth. His teeth in fact were irregular but perfectly white and healthy looking. He wore a winged collar, a black necktie and a dark, sombre suit. He looked like someone of importance in the community. A banker or an undertaker. A merchant banker at the very most. The man behind the counter looked at her with those intensely blue eyes and seemed to register every detail of her appearance with eyes now clouded with sadness. He took her penny and registered it rather grandly on the till and dropped it in the money compartment. It rang hollowly in what must have been a near empty money compartment. One soiled penny with the face of a monarch almost obliterated by hands which had grasped or handled it in its period of existence. And in exchange for which, the man gave her a generously filled cone.

She ate the sugar. All of it. One big cone, an uncommonly generous helping from the stricken man with his radiant eyes. She was sick. Foully sick. The old woman was concerned. She fussed about her. Boiled milk and added the contents of a tuppenny powder which was rotten to take and was called simply 'Cureall'. It was some time before she could retain solids and when she ventured out after her illness and the only affection she had known or was to know from the old woman, she saw that the shop was shuttered and deduced correctly that the man with the intensely blue eyes was dead.

She frequently saw him and he greeted her affectionately when alone. In company he ignored her. Once he passed a coin into her hand. Her hand closed about it and sight unseen, she knew it was half a crown. Silver or reputedly so. Heavy and artistically embossed on one side. The clean features of the King on the other. He smiled and they held hands for a fraction of a second. He winked and nodded towards the railway arch. She nodded consent and was almost sick with excitement. She slipped the coin down a drain. She could not afford to keep it. There was nowhere she could hide it from the woman with her wounded expression and her cold eyes which rarely, if ever, registered happiness or generosity of spirit . . . . Except that once . . . . When she was ill . . . .

The silence was palpable about the shack. The sun totally obscured by the great, unbroken clouds above. There was nothing there. It was empty. Even the sacks had been removed. She gathered he had gone and would never return. Desolation overcame her and she wept and grieved for him because he had brought such warmth and affection into her life.

Unaccountably she thought of Uncle Alex when he returned from one of his business trips to Amsterdam or Brussels or even Paris itself. Impeccably dressed as always. . . in his finest clothes. His darkest and most conservative suit. Shirt immaculately white, a mauve tie and his sartorial glory, a waistcoat of grey, or red, or wine, all embroidered with intertwining stems and leaves and open blossoms of the finest gold thread which glinted so beautifully and alluringly on his protruding waist. And she sat on his lap and traced the intricately entwined stems and leaves and roses, trying to isolate them into single entities. A task which absorbed her to the point of obsession and greatly amused Uncle Alex, because the embroidery was so intricate her task was always futile. Uncle Alex smelling sweetly of some fine quality brilliantine and more faintly of the lavender-scented soap he used daily and a perfume he resorted to from time to time particularly when making visits abroad and he brought her home special gifts, small and possibly inexpensive but which nevertheless charmed and delighted because they were beautifully wrapped in papers of different colours and tied with ribbons of red or white or purple or yellow or gold . . . and inside the small parcels, elegant boxes covered in velvet and containing iced almonds or home-made marzipan sweets and which she treasured and was very reluctant to do the proper thing and politely hand them around and share them with her grandparents and mother. And then Uncle Alex in his tiny patent leather shoes which seemed absurdly small for a man, danced her to bed, talked her to sleep with accounts of his visits to the various cities and their elegant parks and boulevards, their palaces and castles and keeps, museums and art galleries and the rivers which ran through them

which were broad and black and ran with velvet silence and
sheen under the handsome bridges spanning them. Reflecting
as they flowed like diffuse, ill-defined pearls or glittering
diamonds, the lights which were strung along the quays
behind the dark granite bulwarks which contained the
waters. . . . And he kissed her gently and his breath was warm
and sweet and always smelt of peppermints which were a
passion of his and with a surreptitious touch of his plump
jewelled fingers to the inside of thighs he would see her slip
into deep, untroubled sleep. . . . She might wake and hear
them in the next room talking in loud whispers, her nearby
presence forgotten as they anxiously discussed the events in
Germany . . . . Her mother, her Uncle Alex and her grand-
parents from Central Europe whose language she could never
learn or understand and always the subject was of flight
before the onslaught of the Germans, who they were con-
vinced were one day going to cross the frontier to the East
and sweep into the Low Lands. It was one such night she
clearly heard her Uncle Alex instruct her mother to purchase
secretly in small quantities at a time, gold jewellery and
where possible, diamonds. He himself was prepared to allow
her to have some at near cost prices since he dealt in dia-
monds. Her mother was to sew the diamonds and the gold,
pounded flat, carefully inside the lining of her second-best
fur coat. Her best fur coat was all too handsome an affair to
wear under circumstances likely to prevail – someone might
seek to take the coat for its own value – it was very, very
expensive and quite the talk of the town when first she
bought it, and all would be lost. "Alex," her mother declared,
"how clever of you." And for once her voice was neither
brittle or false but full of undisguised admiration. Hearing
them whisper loudly and their shadows cross and recross the
thin strip of light under her bedroom door, she realised
without being told that the tins of meat and fruit – those
at the very back of the storage cupboard – the ones her
mother had packed with such feverish haste on the morning
they had taken flight – contained not fruit or meat but
valuables, all expertly canned by a friend of Alex's who had
a canning factory – and here her mother would touch her
nose with the forefinger of her right hand and exclaim, not

always in sheer admiration — "Alex has a nose for things like that." Which was why he was wealthy and a man respected by the community and which she always failed to understand because her mother loathed Uncle Alex even though he was her brother and she called him vile names and spoke with scorn and the utmost contempt of him and his 'women' . . . and then Boom! and Bang! the diamonds and gold and whatever other valuables there might have been, had all been blown to bits with her mother when a bomb struck the tramp steamer which was bearing her to the safety of England, leaving her abandoned on the quayside. So long ago she couldn't quite remember when . . . .

She awoke suddenly rigid. Nothing disturbed the night's silence which should not disturb it in an area so close to the docks and the river. Yet she sensed their approach . . . the slow, inexorable approach of aircraft intent on death and destruction. Seconds later the sirens sounded. She screamed in terror and saw Uncle Alex's head go plonk, plonk, plonk, along the cobbled street for all the world like a turnip. Fallen from a farmer's cart of turnips on his way to market on market day. The guns stuttered into action and slipping from her bed in the darkened room she peered from behind the blackout blinds and saw the elongated shards which shot from the mouths of the guns and ripped the night sky in their efforts to being down the planes. Frantic searchlights swept the sky in order to illuminate the target of the guns and watching she was astonished how visually beautiful were the means of destruction in modern warfare. The planes continued to approach with an arrogance which was frightening. . . . She heard the throb of their engines and seconds later bombs began to fall and bedlam was loosed all round her.
　　The woman kicked in the bedroom door still frantically dressing. "Come, come come," she shouted and inexplicably she beat her with her fists. "Dress, dress or we will all be killed. Quick, quick," she said and struck her again. She dressed rapidly and bent to button her shoes. The woman screamed at her in fury. "Leave them, leave them. You will get us all killed," and drawing a blanket about her shoulders

she dragged her from the room through the kitchen and down the flight of stairs to where Solly, fully dressed, waited for them with a small battered suitcase. They went outside and saw the sweeping searchlights and heard the stutter of guns and both heard and saw the explosions of bombs as they fell and struck the ground. In the distance, buildings burned, the flames rising high and licking the night sky. There was a fearful beauty about it all and she felt elated and the thought that she or the woman and Solly might be killed never crossed her mind.

Figures dashed about, indistinguishable figures as black against black and then in the light of detonations they were less blackly black and more discernible as human figures. People bumped into one and other and struck out savagely at those they had collided with as if they represented a deadly threat. Somewhere in the darkness a warden shouted at the top of his voice. "Take it easy, take it easy. There's plenty of room for everyone. Don't panic, Don't do Mr bleeding Hitler's work for him." But they paniced and screamed and ran to the nearest shelters which had once looked so fragile and insubstantial and now represented the greatest glory — the chance to survive the inferno in which they were now embroiled. An inferno which was being continuously fed by the bombers which came in wave after wave and against which the anti-aircraft seemed impotent.

She thought of them. Up there. Were they anything like those she had seen on that day when they had fled before the advancing German troops. Were they young and lovely with the simple beauty of youth . . . were they fair and unfulfilled and when they were shot from the sky did they consciously offer their lives in homage to their country and believe that what they were doing was right?

Were they brutal beyond belief,

Heroic beyond measure,

Or did they simply lack imagination?

Rats scurried about their feet . . . piping their terror in high-pitched squeaks which in an odd way reminded her of a very young child in distress or the very old calling for help. There was a human quality about their cries which almost evoked pity.

They gained the entrance to a shelter. The steps were steep and the first impression was of overwhelming dampness. A dim flashlamp was the only source of light. Figures squatted on the benching around the walls like so many people evacuating their bowels in a suspect lavatory. Some clutched children who slept or half slept, their heads rolling to one side in such a manner that it took little imagination to believe those responsible for their welfare had unaccountably, in a moment of aberration, broken their necks, perhaps in the face of the terror all around them. The floor was awash and on its surface floated a doll's head sickeningly lifelike, a child's rattle, some crusts of bread and crushed cigarette nubs. The place was packed to overcrowding and there was an altercation in progress between a smartly dressed man who was accompanied by a young woman who smelt of expensive perfume and who cradled in her arms a baby wrapped in a luxurious blanket. They presented a picture of wealth totally at odds with their surroundings and those, so badly dressed, they wished to shelter amongst. A man, possibly an artisan, with heavy studded boots and corduroy trousers which was held tight at the waist by a wide belt clearly meant for purposes other than the simple support of his trousers, was shouting. He wore a tight but filthy waistcoat which strung across it a chain of silver-like metal which usually went with the cheapest of pocket watches. He was a man of almost heroic stature, the proletarian figure now come to life and shaking his fist and speaking through gritted teeth at the upper-class couple seeking refuge.

"Please," the woman said quietly, her voice heavily accented, "we are refugees from Belgium. We know how you feel." Her voice was soft, pragmatic, above all reasonable . . . the voice of a woman who had never known prejudice of any kind or if she had, had been in the position happily to ignore it.

The man erupted.

"Bleeding Belgians! Cor blimey! Jerry comes at 'em, shoves 'is bayonet up their King's royal arse 'ole and he goes and surrenders without firing a bleedin' shot! Leaving us to all the fighting."

His statement was met with a murmur of general approval. Gentle and low but unmistakably with the potential for savagery and destruction of those impotent before superior forces if once whipped into action. The woman with the child screamed sharply and glanced down to see what had brushed past her. It was a rat, twice as big and as fat as one would imagine one to be. It scurried down the stairs, found itself confronted by water and a group of people stunned into silence by its arrival.

"I'll show you 'ow to treat fucking foreigners. Jews and all!" And with a savage swipe kicked the rat against the concrete wall and followed his first movement by a second one in which he ground underfoot the body of the squealing rat whose entrails spurted through its mouth.

Solly touched the woman lightly and whispered, "Come. We will find shelter somewhere but not here." And in an affectionate gesture he gently stroked the back of the woman's hand. They left the shelter and its occupants vicious with terror and went in search of shelter elsewhere.

They passed a woman struggling with two large, bulging suitcases. She saw them in the glare of blazing buildings and explosions which was now the accepted nightscene. She tugged at the woman's arm. "Here luv, get your old man to give me a hand with these bleeding suitcases and I'll see you right for the night. . . I'm not lying you know. . . I'll see you right as rain 'till morning and no mistake about it. . . I'm Hannie, I am. . . and anyone will tell you Hannie Wetherby's word is as good as gold. Better even." She spoke warmly and in the chill of the night air her voice evoked a warmth in them. Eyes wide in despair the woman took one of the suitcases and lifted it and with an effort carried it along with the small, battered suitcase Solly had given her to carry. Solly with his bad chest could not be expected to carry anything. He coughed and beat his chest and turned his head aside at regular intervals and spat on the pavement and because he thought it was good manners, he ground the phlegm underfoot and then dogtrotted until, wheezing more than ever, he caught up with them. She walked beside the others feeling vibrantly alive as she had been before. She experienced no feelings of fear but was awestruck at the majesty of a city being compelled to devour itself. The mixture of colour in the flames and the rising smoke and of the blazing guns and exploding bombs fascinated and intrigued her by their various colours and hues and startling colour combinations. She experienced what was almost ecstasy with each detonation and the sound of an aircraft screaming as it fell blazing to inevitable destruction on the ground aroused in her lower stomach curiously sexual feelings and the teasing desire to pass water.

Above loomed the railway with its massive arches spanning a mean huddle of houses, small back yards and some waste ground. The recesses between the high arches were deep and though crowded they weren't full and those sheltering there lacked the bristling, provocative hostility of those in the other shelter. "Here we are luv. All safe and sound. Safe as houses we are here. Safe as the bleeding Bank of England." Mrs Wetherby laughed uproariously at her own words and showed a mouth with pink, hardened gums and the black stubs of what were once teeth. The jollity in her voice evoked warmth and trust. She nudged the woman who had carefully laid down the heavy suitcase. "Told you, didn't I? Told you that Hannie Wetherby's word is worth its weight in bleeding gold." The woman smiled faintly and nodded her head gratefully and seemed for once human. Solly beamed and thumped and turned and spat on the ground, grinding the spittle underfoot. The walls of the shelter were whitewashed to a height about four times as high as the average man. The woman they could now plainly see was fat and wedged in clothing which seemed far too small for her great bulk. Her chin was lost in the folds of flesh hanging from the lower half of her face. Her eyes were small like those of a piglet but shone in warm, vulgar good humour. Her upper-arms were like the thighs of the average woman and her immense body was a mass of flesh which rippled and shook with every movement she made. Her entire weight was carried by two stumpy legs disproportionately small, as were her ankles and her feet which were wedged into canvas runners, cut in places to allow carbuncles to show through in comfort. "My bleeding Billy's here," she said to no one

in particular. . . "or should be. Wouldn't be surprised if the
bleeder isn't having it off with some little tart he's managed
to pick up. I don't know what it is with youngsters these
days. It wasn't like that in my day, I can tell you that. . . .
If you wasn't no virgin on your wedding night your mother
would want to know all about it." She sighed and her entire
upper body moved with difficulty. "Still, what with this
bleeding war and all, I can't say I blame them. Take what
you can while you can. . . that's what I always say . . . .
And I know his bleeding father did. Couldn't get enough he
couldn't. Very passionate nature he had. Could tell from his
eyes. Still, I don't complain. It wasn't that I didn't enjoy
it. . . I did. . . . Never refused him I didn't even if it came on
him while I was doing the Sunday roast. I'm pleased about
that, I can tell you, seeing how he went and died so sudden."
She turned to the woman who was flushing slightly and
gazing with great concentration at the toes of her shoes.
"Wait here luv and I'll have a peep around and then I'll
see you settled down for the night. . . . See if I don't."

And leaving them in possession of her two bulging suit-
cases she ambled off and was lost to sight. They felt cons-
cious under the relentless eyes of those lying around like
corpses laid out on the plot of earth in which they were
to be later interred. In the background someone started
to play a harmonica. She didn't recognise the music but
it was low and sad and suggested suffering. "Here mate,"
a man shouted. "Why not play the bleeding dead march
from 'Saul' while you're at it?" "That's right," someone
bellowed in agreement. "Play something to cheer us up."
The demand was echoed by a chorus of others all demand-
ing something to cheer them up. The music of the harmonica
faltered and ceased abruptly. "What's up now?" the original
objector demanded. "I don't know anything bleeding cheer-
ful, that's what!" the man with the harmonica snarled. "God
Almighty, he don't know anything cheerful," the objector
snorted in contempt. "Play something by our Gracie," a
woman suggested quietly. "She's ever so nice is our Gracie. . . .
I like Gracie. I love Gracie," she continued as if intent on a
litany of glory. "Fuck Gracie," a woman shouted. "I wouldn't
half mind if I could," another man shouted and there was

general laughter and a woman could be heard above the
laughter as she affected what she considered a superior accent
and said, "What language to use in front of ladies, I must say."
"Bugger this," a woman shouted, "from the stink around
here its easy to know you lot can shit a lot better than you
can sing. Well, I can do both and I'm not ashamed of neither,"
and without drawing breath she started to sing, 'My Old
Man said follow the band,' and immediately her song was
taken up by virtually all present. The harmonica player join-
ed in and an accordion player and she was surrounded by
what had once so appealed to her when first she had come to
England. The sound of round, jolly voices singing round,
jolly tunes when the evenings were quiet and everything limp
after the day's heat. A jollity she had never known before
and which contrasted starkly with those rare occasions when
the family met in what was supposed to be a happy gathering
and turned instead into a chill ritual of exact politeness which
killed all hope of fun or enjoyment and her grandmother sang
thrillingly in some Western Russian dialect a song of the
earth and love and survival and her mother played 'La Mere'
with surprising sympathy and technique and she herself
sang 'The Maiden's Prayer' which she didn't really like,
while her mother accompanied her on the piano, much to
Uncle Alex's delight who had taught her the song and in-
variably demanded it. Why she never knew since it induced
melancholy in him and, moist-eyed, he promptly withdrew
into himself and took no further part in the proceedings
whatever they might be. . . religious or purely social.

The song came to an end. There was a lull during which
could be heard the din of a city under continual bombard-
ment from the sky. "Are we afraid of Mister fucking 'Itler?"
demanded someone in a loud bellow. "No! We fucking well
are not!" retorted the crowd in unison and then laughter
splintered the common bond and they were once more so
many individuals or family groups seeking shelter and, if
possible, safety.

A figure shuffled out of the darkness. It was Mrs Wether-
by. She was breathing deeply and with difficulty and when
caught by reflected light, her brow could be seen to be film-
ed with sweat which to her smelt pleasantly warm in a

motherly way. She had traces of a moustache above her upper lip and beads of sweat hung there like the dew drops she had seen on grasses and sedges and the cobwebs strung between the branches of low-lying shrubs in the fields and ditches about the village in which she was born so long ago she couldn't quite remember when. . . . Mrs Wetherby wiped her brow with an irregular piece of cloth cut from a calico dress or apron. Watching the woman she was conscious of warmth and an infinity of spirit she could never hope to find in the woman who looked after her. The other lacked this woman's warm and generous sense of the matriarchal to which she could respond. The other woman sensed as much. She reached a hand forward and stroked her on the head and then slipping her hand under the hair at the nape of her neck she pinched her painfully and vindictively causing her to cry out. "Poor child," the woman said stroking her hair again. "She is so, so, tired. . . and she eats so little." Mrs Wetherby clucked sympathetically.

Another figure came shuffling in out of the darkness. It was a boy of fourteen or so with a very pallid skin and small, sharp eyes and hair heavily oiled and carefully combed back.

"There you are, you silly little bugger," Mrs Wetherby exclaimed with undisguised delight and pride. "Had enough for one night have you? Or is it still tingling?" He grinned broadly and made no effort to reply because no reply was expected. He was tall and gangly and his trousers didn't hang quite properly. The sleeves of his jacket were too short and showed his hands above the knuckle. He kept his head bowed as if boyishly shy and smiled a perpetual smile of secretive amusement. His hair could be seen to be fair, darkened by the cheap brilliantine he used to keep it swept back and which smelt both harshly and unpleasantly.

"Where's your bleeding manners?" Mrs Wetherby demanded in the worshipping tones. "Cat got your tongue or something?" He muttered "Howyedo" and the woman inclinced her head in a practised bow of acknowledgement and Solly muttered "Hello" and coughed and realised there was nowhere he could safely spit and swallowed his spittle instead. She simply nodded and for an instance he raised his head and she saw his eyes were large and luminous and he had a quick and ready smile which, far from being shy, was blatantly sexual in a free and easy manner.

Dropping his eyes again and gripping the suitcases and leaving his mother to carry her own, he took one of hers and Solly's battered one and went ahead of them towards the towering areas of black silhouetted against the night sky, lit by several fires roaring, flaming and vying for one's attention. Above aircraft came on and on, their engines throbbing smoothly, innocently so, as though they were not in fact responsible for the carnage below them.

They crushed green grass and they could smell it pungent and fresh despite the warm, acrid air which billowed about and which brought grit and hot ash towards them. Farther on there was the unmistakable smell of excrement strongly smelling chemicals couldn't quite obliterate.

"That's the lav down there," Mrs Wetherby informed them. "Try and go in the day. Then it's not too bad. Some around here are a dirty lot of buggers what don't know how to behave themselves. Shit themselves anywhere they would, even in their own parlours. Too bleeding lazy, see, to go all the way down there in the dark, so they just squat wherever they like and do whatever they have to do. Dangerous in the dark. Could easily slip and do yourself an injury."

She paused and drew breath for some seconds and then moved on to what was plainly another series of railway arches. She passed a few openings which had sacking or tarpaulin across the lower half of their entrances. Like sweat, those inside exuded fear as if it were a bodily secretion one could both smell and see. She ducked behind one of the tarpaulins announcing "This is ours," unconscious of her arrogant use of the possessive. Inside, the darkness was punctured by the glowing tips of cigarettes.

"It's Hannie," a chorus greeted her arrival. Like a regal figure she stood inside the entrance and, just about visible in the glow from the sky, she remained standing and raised a hand in a queenly manner and graciously named a few friends who were somewhere in there in the darkness she couldn't come to terms with just yet. "Flo, Ada, Kate and Lucy...." All responded eagerly to her greeting as if singularly honoured. Unmistakably there was, however, affection in their voices and in some cases gratitude. She walked down an aisle between rows of blankets which were laid on the stone floor of the arch, each marking the undisputed territory of those who owned the blanket, whether or not they were occupied, and piled about them were whatever their owners thought necessary for the night. Some had thermos flasks wrapped in clothing or newspapers and nestling safely in straw baskets. Others had a few corked lemonade bottles full of tea well diluted by milk and very likely with sugar added. Other baskets or carriers contained what she rightly assumed to be food of some kind or another. Bodily comfort was the object of the entire arrangement and, surprisingly, what they would have once considered a barbaric way of living, unfitting for humans, they now accepted with remarkable ease underwritten by an unspoken, unbreakable resistance.

She was used to the darkness which wasn't altogether unbroken. The entire night sky was illuminated by the many fires and, penetrating the tarpaulin covering the front of the arch, a faint, green-hued light seeped through. Luridly the high curved vault of the arch reflected the dancing flames outside and was a further source of weak, reflected light. She could now easily discern the various aisles between the blankets and the huddled figures on some, whispering softly to one another. Others sought oblivion in sleep and most of those were men who would be expected at work the following morning. Some young couples made tentative love and other solitary forms lay prone, their folded arms serving as a pillow while they stared ahead at nothing in particular, or drew hungrily on cigarettes cupped in the palms of their hands.

Some women squatted or knelt by an old woman who was propped up on a mattress with blankets folded about her to waist-level while her head rested on a bundle of clothing which served as a pillow. Incongruously she wore a bright blue nightdress and a blue knitted shawl about her shoulders. She had silver white hair carefully attended to and imperfect but clean teeth. Lively blue eyes, a stubby nose and a generous mouth. Her skin was flawless and only the green-hued light distorted what was almost the beauty of the contentedly aged. She obviously commanded the affection and attentions of those about her.

Mrs Wetherby ambled over to pay her respects.

"How are we today luv? No nasty turns? No bad pains?"

The woman answered in a voice startlingly free of dialect of any kind. It was soft and silver-toned, resonant and clear, without affectation of any kind, further enhancing her appearance.

"A slight turn Hannie love. But I got over it."

"Feeling better then? Can't have you taken bad like that, now can we?"

"I'm much better Hannie. Thank you."

Unconsciously Mrs Wetherby extended a pudgy hand and stroked the woman's gleaming hair, the language of unspoken love. "I have your little treat for you," she said. "I'll be over when things are a little more private like and give it to you." The woman smiled radiantly.

"Thank you Hannie. And God bless you."

Mrs Wetherby ambled back to them.

"That's our Lill," she said proudly. "Been in service with the quality all her life and not a bit stuck up about it neither. You can tell by the way she keeps herself, can't you? As neat as a pin and as clean as a new born baby. And the way she talks! Lovely the way she talks without being hoity-toity about it. As I always say, you can't work with paint without some of it rubbing off on you."

She led them to the back of the arch which was partially bricked up and had obviously been used as a storage place for timber at one time or another. There was a smell of sawdust which permeated the air and mingled with the smell of glue and resin and was welcomingly refreshing. She pulled back a curtain which neatly sectioned off the area she had claimed, on both sides, affording her the greatest privacy in the entire place.

"This is our dump," she said denigratingly but not altogether without pride. In a cutaway tin a small night-light burned, its light meagre and incapable of being seen from outside. It lent a cheerful glow to what otherwise might have been a depressing scene. Neatly laid out on the dusty concrete

floor were two rubber sheets on which were two single
mattresses. Nearby was positioned a small cupboard on which
stood two china cats of the kind frequently found on a
mantlepiece of a kitchen in the district. A primus stove stood
in a metal box of sand, the front of the box being cut away
to allow the use of the stove as it stood. On the wall hung a
pot, a pan and a tin basin, an exact replica of the one the
woman used to wash herself in ritually every morning. The
sight of such snug arrangements aroused envy in her.

Mrs Wetherby took out a thermos from a hidden basket
and poured them some tea into chipped cups. The woman
drew a sharp breath and seemed about to refuse the offered
cup. She had an obsessive hatred of dirt rooted in her Jewish
background and would never at home tolerate the presence
of a cracked or broken cup. She stifled her cry of horror and
smiled a bright, false smile and nodded her head in gratitude.
She touched her breast with her hand in a delicate movement
and murmured obsequiously, "You are so kind, so kind." Yet
there was calculation and cunning in her voice. "Cheers," said
Mrs Wetherby. "And bugger 'Itler and all the rest of them
bleeding Germans." They drank the tea without responding
to the toast. Mrs Wetherby sat on an upturned crate, her
great bulk spreading out on all sides completely covering the
crate. She looked reflective as she sipped the tea which was
strong and bitter, without additive of any kind.

"There was some tried to keep Hannie from staking her
claim to this here little place. The police for one. Tried to
move me on they did the first night I come her." She tossed
her head and mimiced a policeman to perfection. "'This 'ere
place is not a public shelter madam. It isn't designated a
shelter for the simple reason it's constructed throughout of
bricks. Bricks madam and mortar. It wouldn't require a direct
hit to bring this place crashing down on top of you with fatal
consequences ... a bomb dropped within a thousand yards
would do that,' he said full of his own bleeding importance.
'How's that?' I say, pretending I was shit ignorant. Well, I
mean there are times when you have to. 'Blast waves madam,
the secondary effect of a bomb ... sufficient to bring this
entire structure down from a distance of a thousand feet. I'm
afraid you can't stay here. I'll have to move you on.''' Mrs

Wetherby paused and smiled and showed her rotten teeth. "'Move on?' says I. 'Where to? Back to me bleeding house in Victoria Street . . . . Do you know what that's made of hofficer?' I asked. 'Bricks. Bleeding bricks and mortar. Nothing bleeding else. And half the bleeding street's gone if you want to know. You want me to go back so they can finish me off with the rest of the houses. Not bleedin likely. You nor no one like you is shifting Hannie Wetherby not once she's made up her mind!' And that set him back no end I can tell you. There were others come out here after me and soon they were all crowding around him and it nearly turned into a riot . . . so in the end he just tucked his tail under his hind legs and slung off like a beaten hound. And I should think so and all. Made them put in the lavatories we did after a while and give us the canvas to cover the fronts of the arches. I mean, if we're going to stay here we might as well be comfortable. That's what I said."

And she smacked her lips hugely and smiled a broad, roguish smile full of self satisfaction.

"So kind, so kind," the woman exclaimed softly and sipped her tea as though it were gall.

"There's a place there at the back . . . it don't get too much light and it's a bit cold, that's why it hasn't been taken. You go in there luv and we'll see about fixing it up for you. All it needs is a bit of himagination and it'll be home from home like my little place is."

She led them there and their hearts sank. The air was chilled like the air in the more opulent vaults in the village graveyard she had sometimes played in when she was younger. Her excursions into those cheerless structures had largely been the results of the dares of other children and were only possible because Uncle Alex had solemnly assured her that, contrary to rumour, the dead were without feeling or power of any kind whatever and that all ghost stories were utter rubbish. Fortified by those assurances once inside a vault she had been able to count aloud to one hundred prefixing each number with the word 'and' . . . one and two and three, and despite the other children wailing and throwing clods of earth onto the roof of the vault, she had remained and successfully braved her fears of all such places. The incident she recalled gave her a certain status amongst those she played with. No others had dared equal her feat.

"I'll let you have an oil sheet for tonight . . . I can see you brought blankets." The woman nodded quickly. She had in fact brought one. "That should see you through the night and we'll see about going to your place and making this place more comfortable. A home from home — like mine." The woman again nodded gratefully and the boy laid down their very insubstantial suitcase and with a quick dart in her direction, he smiled faintly with what was meant to appear as touching shyness and then with a quick movement of the right hand and a backward toss of his head, he brushed back into position the long hank of hair above his forehead and left them.

Mrs Weatherby surveyed the scene. "It's not much is it? Still, you'll be safe here . . . safe as the Bank of England," she said with sublime confidence. "Nobody's going to bomb Hannie Weatherby . . . nobody is," she added as if after being bombed she would be in a position to object strongly and in person to the German Chancellor. "Things will soon pick up when you've got your few bits and pieces about you . . . wait and see if I'm wrong."

The woman again struck her breast lightly in what was fast becoming familiar ritual. "You are so kind, so kind."

"Give us a shout when you are finished with the cups . . . just call and you can hand them over the curtain . . . and if there's anything I can give you . . . you just ask. Hannie Weatherby never said no to people what's genuine and never will," and smiling broadly, she ambled off and they distinctly heard her shuffle down the aisle and engage Lill in conversation.

The woman sighed and gritted her teeth and as if confronted by the ruins of the temple for the first time and having known it in its glory, she muttered, "Oihya, oihya, oihya," and very audibly struck her sunken chest as if overwhelmed by the desolation by which she found herself surrounded. Solly coughed and cleared his throat and said, "It's better than water and dirty things in the water and dirty goys squabbling with one and other . . . and rats," he repeated for emphasis, "rats."

"Yes," she said in that high, whining voice which was so

characteristic of her . . . the whine of one defeated by life and living, the voice of one who saw death as the great surcease. "Yes," she said dully, "it's better than rats." But not very much more, her tone implied.

She laid out the single blanket on the oilcloth on the floor and fully clothed all three lay down and lay under it and tried to overcome their repugnance of sleeping with one another. She laid next to the woman and thought her breath is sweet but her skin smells of onion and lying rigidly like one coffined she tried to avoid all unnecessary contact with the thin woman whose bones were sharp and protruding.

Against the clamour of many people whispering and the outrages of the city under bombardment, she drifted into sleep. At one time during the night she heard a high-pitched voice call out "Can Billy come out and play Mrs Wetherby?" and Mrs Wetherby's voice which betrayed that even one so easy going and as tolerant as she, had her limitations, "No, he can not you dirty little bitch. He's had enough for one night and so have you. If you want a poke ask a bleeding copper." To the girl's low moan was added the boy's voice high in indignation. "Ah Mum," and then unmistakably the sound of a fleshy hand striking a fleshy cheek and smiling at the inoffensive vulgar good humour she drifted in sleep and dreamt about the Müllers and the young Mrs Müller who was so many years younger than Mr Müller who was gross and fat and had sickeningly thick, protruding lips, the lower one of which was lax and exposed his lower gum and teeth. He sweated a lot and drooled also and used quite a lot of finely washed and ironed handkerchiefs a day and even seeing him as a dream figure she wondered as she always had in reality, why so beautiful and so young a woman as Mrs Müller had married so old and ugly a man as her husband and why, despite their considerable wealth, the Müllers were not received in the best social circles of the village or the country about it where many industrialists from the city had their country retreats.

He kicked the toe of his shoe against the wall, his voice heavy with frustration. "Ah come on," he pleaded. "A walk, just a walk . . . I won't do nothing, I promise." And the falsity of his promises was evident even to her who still had great difficulty in understanding English, relying more on intuition rather than complete understanding of the language whenever anyone spoke to her. She shook her head in refusal. He again kicked at the wall and his plea took on a new urgency and she thought that, unlike his mother who wasn't very conscientious when it came to personal hygiene, his body was fresh and smelt of greenery in spring or after a shower of rain. His breath, though the upper reaches of his teeth were scaled, was sweet and fragrant, and had a freshness of its own which was not unattractive.

"No," she repeated, shaking her head to emphasise what she had already emphasised by her tone.

"A walk. Just a bleeding walk. For five flipping minutes." His voice was that of someone about to weep. It was full and plaintive, hung with beggary and, she noted, a certain calculation.

His eyes were grey and not pale blue as first she thought, and in his pupils were flecks of straw-gold. Here beggary was at its rifest. Here the vulnerability underlying his pleas was naked and winning.

"Alright," she said. "But don't tell the woman."

He understood immediately what she meant. "You mean that piss-eyed weasel what stops with you and the old bloke?" She nodded, feeling his description though harsh was apt. "Got a face like a cat's arse that one."

Curiously Mrs Wetherby seemed to feel she had a certain charm. She went everywhere with the old woman and when introduced to strangers smiled benevolently, muttering, "So kind, so kind," and tugged at the end of the sleeves of her cardigan like a shy but winsome schoolgirl. She accompanied her on her visits to Lill when most of those in the shelter were snatching what sleep they could and was privileged to be present when Mrs Wetherby spooned a few drops of whisky into Lill's parched throat and received the inevitable benediction, "God bless you love — you're a lady." And Mrs Wetherby screamed in what for her was subdued laughter. "Hark at her! Me a flipping lady!" And as though gelatinous, her huge fleshy bulk shivered in unison with her laughter. The old woman smiled a wintery smile and obtained a reputation of a woman of some grace and gentility. Her attitude, though more furtively vindictive, remained the same.

"Where are you going?" she asked him, when after a few faltering steps he slipped his hand into hers and tried to affect the manners of an older young man. "There's a cutting down the line. It's deserted. They don't use it any more. It's got a bleeding guard room — well, more a house really, and it's got a small bed. The flipping place is as bare as a baby's arse but upstairs it's got a bed with the lot . . . mattress, blankets . . . pillow and even sheets. And quite oblivious of the fact he had betrayed his true intentions, he squeezed her hand affectionately.

"What," she asked curiously, "is a cutting?"

He shrugged his shoulders and glanced at her in what could only be described as pity. "I keep forgetting you're a foreigner. You don't know English like us." He hesitated. "Well, it's a bit like this. Rails and sleepers and points and switches and things like that. It's a place where they used to shunt trains up there off the main line. Coal I suppose. Or something like it. The place is filthy dirty, I can tell you that for nothing . . . See, by shunting off the goods trains off up there they could keep the trains running on the main line without having to stop while the others were being unloaded." He stopped, his powers of explanation exhausted. He glanced at her. "Understand what I mean?" She nodded and smiled though she hadn't understood at all. He steered her across the wide stretch of crossings and soon they were on a broad, cindered track overgrown with weeds, which curved gently and passed directly under a series of arches like those they used for shelter farther down the track. They passed a series of warehouses, big patterns of dark against the night sky and the evening darkness, a darkness of deep, velvet blue, not the black pitch of night, star studded. She squeezed his hand in fear, remembering the black-haired man who had so loved her and had been brutally murdered. She remembered the sunshine, the brilliance of beaten gold, his splendid body curled asleep on the sacking in the centre of the floor of the hut, its timbers wheaten in the sunlight.

He misinterpreted her increased pressure as a gesture of

affection. He stopped and turned to her and kissed her quickly on the lips. His hand moved up the broad of her back and then moved rapidly until they were between her thighs exploring them in small circular movements. His hand was soft and unhardened for one supposed to be training as a sheet metal worker. He bit her on the lobe of one ear, his hand sought her vagina and finding clutched it with all four fingers and thumb of one hand and played softly on it inducing the secretions already beginning to flow with all the sweet pain they had first flown under the expert excitation of the black-haired man, now dead.

"Here," he said, alarmed at the swiftness of her response and possibly his own. "We can't bleeding do it here like you was a bitch in heat."

And laughingly, tipping her tongue to his, they broke apart. He moved quickly and expertly despite the advancing darkness and guided her through a labyrinth of high, abandoned warehouses and single-storied railway buildings scattered all over an area covered with criss-crossing tracks until they reached what he called the guard house. It was a mean but solidly built, two-storied house with two rooms on ground level, two above. He ushered her inside and quickly bolted the sturdy door. Breathing with difficulty he led her upstairs and into a small room. He struck a match and lit a candle in a cutaway can of familiar workmanship and design, which stood on a bedside chair. He checked the blackout curtains and at last felt free to breathe easily. She glanced at the bed neatly made, the top of its sheets and blankets turned down as if used daily. He was tense and anxious when he spoke. "For Christ sake get undressed. Jerry'll be here soon, and I don't want to get mine. Not in this dirty little kip."

She undressed and he stood to examine her in great detail. Then, unsmiling, he began to undress. With a masculine pride he stroked his penis. "It's bigger than most," he muttered and she wondered how he could possibly know. They slipped into bed and she found his movements were timorous and explorative, lacking the direct aggressive authority she had expected of one with his reputation. He kissed her about the throat and ears and bit her on the nape of her neck and on her right shoulder but seemed reluctant to mount. She took his member freely in her hand and moulded it between her fingers. He groaned softly and began an assault of kisses and bites and rough caresses and she continued to stimulate him until finally she parted her legs and tucked them slightly up and, groaning through gritted teeth, he penetrated.

The sirens sounded and instinctively they both knew they sounded more urgent, more menacing than usual.

"Christ Almighty," he muttered as he sought frantically to complete his penetration and climax. She slipped her hand behind his back and with the full force of her body pulled him towards her and the same time upwards while she thrust downward with all her might. Now he abandoned all efforts at restraint and any consideration he might have for her as an individual. He sought only to reach the innermost regions of her lower body and, as ordained, spill his seed. Her moans were half pleasure, half pain. Unconsciously she dug her nails into the broad of his back and drew a line downwards, incising on his unblemished skin a thin, red streak which remained pencil thin for some seconds and then became more diffused and less well defined as it bled. His body tensed to the utmost for a second, he maintained his position and then in a series of spasm, his body shuddered and he spilled. She clasped her hands and thighs about him preventing his withdrawal. She laughed lightly and bit his lower lip drawing some blood and was amazed how dormantly the greed of her entrails and her lower body had remained since she had last been with him . . . the man with the jet black hair which in a certain light could be seen to be tinted blue and green like the feathers of a raven. With a struggle he withdrew and turned on his back and lay panting. His entire body was covered with sweat and she saw his chest rise and fall, his ribs easily visible, and thought how boyish he was and how under-nourished. She remained unmoving by him, reluctant to be the one to break the silence. He turned towards her and said almost petulantly and accusative, "I'll tell you this for nothing. You're no fucking virgin. You've had it before. And you liked it," and somehow there was a sense of wound in his voice, but whether it was because he hadn't been the first to lie with her or because she had enjoyed it she couldn't be sure. Suddenly they heard a high-pitched whine. He threw himself over her without hesitation. They both knew it was going to be close. The only question was, how close. It fell to earth some distance away. The entire building shook and they heard distinctly the sound of slates slipping in profusion from the roof and shattering as they struck the ground. Again they heard the high-pitched whine and now they clutched one another in sheer terror. It dropped even closer. Part of the roof caved in and the wall opposite crumbled as though made of nothing more than under-fired red bricks. Panting, he struggled into his trousers.

"Come on," he urged, "they're getting too close for fucking comfort." She swung her body over the edge of the bed and began to dress. They could now hear the steady drone of aircraft engines. She knew they were directly in the flight path of a number of bombers. Six or even eight. Or even twelve. It didn't really matter. Each would drop their string of bombs and their chances of survival if they went outside were slight. Inside they had a chance . . . a very slim chance. It was unwise of them to flee. She longed to tell him but lacked sufficient English to do so.

She struggled into her shoes and had difficulty with the button of one. Otherwise she was fully dressed. He grabbed her by the hand. "Come on, don't fucking bother about that!" And then they were outside running and on all sides of them buildings were crumbling and some had caught fire and the fire consumed them with an appetite that was astonishing. At least a century old, their timber was bone dry and cracked audibly as they burned. Smoke billowed everywhere and tiny cinders, mere specks of burning wood, rained down on them threatening above all their eyes and hair. Despite the chaos about her she could smell the pungent smell of burning hair. Frantically she tore at her head to prevent her hair from catching fire. They broke free and both were having difficulty in breathing. Every time they inhaled they inhaled smoke and cinders and, it seemed, living flame. They heard it again . . . the high-pitched whine, and knew it would be closest of all. She stumbled and fell. He turned and seeing her and unable to shout he waved her forward with his arms. Before she could move he had turned and ran on ahead. The bomb fell and exploded nearby ... though not as near as she had dreaded. She saw him running on, seeking the shelter of a ware-house still intact and untouched by fire. To her horror from her vantage point she saw the top of the building begin to topple even as he reached what he believed to be its protection. In a moment he was lost under the heap of falling building blocks of some hardstone or other. Dust churned everywhere. She rose, intending to take flight. Something struck her a glancing blow. She fell forward and lost consciousness.

Part II

Part II

GERTRUDE

She saw Billy run forward and the building collapse. Then she was confronted by the mass of rubble which had been the railway arches and under which both Solly, the woman, Mrs Wetherby and close on a hundred people had perished when the arches had received a direct hit. She screamed a low, soft scream which rose in pitch and volume and went on and on, and then Gertrude shook her lightly by the arm and kissing her lightly on the cheek said, "Good morning my love. It's gone ten already and such a perfectly beautiful morning I felt I couldn't let you sleep any longer."

Her voice was crisp and brisk and, as always, quietly authoritative if not indeed totalitarian as she spoke and partially pulled back the curtains fully lifting the blinds, flooding the room with strong, white sunshine, which at first she found blinding.

"Was I having nightmares again?" she asked timidly afraid she had woken Gertrude with her screaming as she had done so often in the past.

Gertrude considered. "Unpleasant dreams I should say rather than outright nightmares. Can't you remember any of the details?"

She did. In startling clarity but lied and said "No."

"Just as well," said Gertrude briskly and going out to the landing brought in the breakfast tray she had left on the small table positioned on the landing by the door specifically for that purpose. She carried the tray in processional splendour which her superbly erect carriage enabled her to do, and deftly positioned it on her knees in the bed.

On the tray reposed rather than lay, an egg, bacon crisply

65

done, sausages, toast, honey in a pot and a single rose . . . red with petals which looked like velvet and just about to unfurl further, not quite to the point, however, when for her, roses in particular became brash and somewhat vulgar.

Gertrude watched her anxiously.

She realised as much and enthused as expected. "Perfect . . . . And the rose. . . . Superb! I couldn't ask for anything better."

Gertrude beamed and clasped her hands before her in a self-congratulatory gesture, the unconscious gesture of those who take infinite pains to please others in small matters, and said, "Believe it or not, I plucked it this morning when the dew was still on it and everything else for that matter . . . but unfortunately it dried before I had prepared the toast." She laughed the silvery toned laugh which characterised her and complemented her almost perfect beauty of body and mind. "It's just as well really. It would have been all too theatrical for words."

She bit a piece of toast. Melted butter ran down her chin. "Delicious," she murmured. "And the rose . . . I hope you kept the really perfect ones for . . . " She froze, the butter trickled down down her fingers and she stared sightlessly on the rose so deeply red it seemed to encapsulate a torrent of blood.

Gertrude bowed her head momentarily and gulped slightly and clasped her hands in an almost prayerful attitude. "Yes my dear . . . I've kept the most beautiful for David . . . you don't mind . . . do you?" Tears ran down her face and she made no effort to staunch them.

She looked levelly at her. "You know perfectly well I don't mind in the slightest. It was stupid and unthoughtful of me to mention them." She stretched a hand forward and Gertrude approached and clasped her hand and because she wanted it and felt Gertrude wanted it with a desire which was raw and rank and felt shameful for harbouring such desire while David, dead and as yet uncoffined, lay in his bed upstairs. . . . She shoved aside the tray and brushed against Gertrude's upper body. Her lips sought and found hers as they kissed in the prolonged manner which so pleased them. She took Gertrude's hands and laid them on her breasts.

Gertrude stroked them lovingly and gently and then as her desire increased, less gently, less softly, Gertrude laughed, or rather snorted shortly, and then clasped her to her bosom and laying her head on hers she wept freely for the first time since David had died with nothing more than the faintest of exhalation . . . a soft, low moan which to her as she had heard it, seemed to signify the pity of the world.

"What am I to do Anna? What am I to do? . . . I know it sounds unbearably cruel and selfish but he was my life . . . he was everything I ever had until I met you. . . . It was and is selfish and even wrong to think that one should have more than one happiness in life when so many experience little or no happiness at all. . . . But you and he were all I ever wanted under any circumstances whatever . . . and now . . . I can't believe he's gone."

Quickly she pushed aside the tray and slipped from the bed. She took Gertrude by the hand and led her to her bedroom where the bed was already made, the room fully prepared. Here and only here Gertrude could make love without qualm or inhibition.

She undid the bow at her neck and shed the light nightdress, exposing her body fully and relishing the intense hunger and desire the sight of her firm body aroused in Gertrude's eyes. Gertrude turned aside murmuring to herself, "Not yet . . . not yet. . . ."

She spoke and her voice had a firmness she couldn't quite credit. "He's been dead for three days. And you haven't wept or loved or laughed. You must begin again. Remember what you said when you visited me in hospital in London? You said, 'However painful the past, you must forget it or it will extend the tyranny of the grave into your daily life and dictate your every action, no matter where you choose to go in an effort to avoid it.' Please, Gertrude . . . please let's make love."

Gertrude nodded and slipped out of her clothing and lay upon her back on the bed and spreading her legs proffered her vagina, already beginning its slight pulsations. She knelt and slipped off Gertrude's stockings and shoes and when the form on the bed was quite naked she clambered over her body and pressing firmly down on her, she kissed her with a raw, startling hunger and bit her lightly on the neck and breasts and then entwining her feet about one of Gertrude's, her own vagina beginning to secrete, she knelt and with increasing greed and mounting passion she feasted fully on what was freely offered to her.

And unrestrainedly Gertrude wept for the frail, reduced body of David her brother, once her lover.

She continued to probe and lick and penetrate with her tongue as fully as she could until Gertrude began to squirm with passion and now more fully aroused, her thoughts succumbed to the flesh at its most aroused. She climaxed and uttered a low cry of both pleasure and betrayal and wept again but this time more softly, more humanly and stroked Anna's hair as she knelt there depleted, her head burrowed into the warmth of the thighs she loved. And Anna relishing each stroke, each "thank you my love, thank you", which Gertrude murmured from time to time in a tone of almost inexpressible gratitude, and Anna in turn wept, deeply moved that an act of love on her part should elicit such expressions of love.

Sunlight drenched the room and fell slantingly on the light-coloured carpet, the bed and the naked bodies sprawled on its edge. In it moved motes of dust which, viewed through tears, appeared to be encircled with all the colours of the rainbow in prismatic progression as they moved restlessly, entrancingly, like untutored but enchanted dancers.

The doorbell rang loudly and persistently with unwarranted firmness. There was unconscious arrogance in the persistent pressure on the ivory button of the brass doorbell to the right of the doorway to the porch. "Damn," said Gertrude, "it's that bloody man the vicar. Only he'd persist in such a manner." Her face contorted with rage and as always was ugly in rage. Her eyes flashed spitefully and her voice was serrated with vindictiveness. "What the hell has he come for?" she asked, scrambling frantically about for her clothing, ". . . to prove that he's not merely the Vicar of Christ but the Christ himself? Will he display the wounds of his hands and feet? Not to speak of those of his body? Those unspeakable

Christians and their worship of a Semite of doubtful historical authenticity to say the least, and who, if he ever existed, would in my opinion, have had foul breath." She dressed and tugged at the back of her skirt. "Am I straight behind?"

She nodded, and satisfied, Gertrude sallied forth to meet, though not necessarily to greet, Mr Chuckleworth, the vicar of the parish church of Saint James the Greater. In the short distance to the door it crossed her mind that once, when Father was alive and David and Mother ... that ghostly insubstantial figure who drifted mist-like into life and departed similarly, leaving heartache and otherwise vague impressions like breath blown upon a window pane, they used to treck to Saint James on his feast-day and hear Mr Chuckleworth preach a sermon on the saint, giving the distinct impression that if truth and justice prevailed Saint James the Greater, not Christ, would have been slung on the cross for both vilification — a Christian joy according to Mr Chuckleworth — and veneration. Mother amused them by observing that so unconsciously a snob was the vicar, he would by chance if encountering Saint James the Lesser (assuming there was one) in all his celestial glory, pass him by on the assumption that being the Lesser, he was also inferior, and therefore not worth knowing.

She stopped at the door and turned, her hand on the doorknob and already beginning to turn it. "Do get dressed darling and have breakfast if it's still fit for human consumption and then come on down and deliver me from the feathering old fellow."

Mrs Platt met her in the hall and with the sense of sorrow and injury she so loved to hug and cultivated so assiduously, informed her that the vicar, Mr Chuckleworth, was in the study and wished to have a word with her if it wasn't at all too inconvenient. Having imparted the message Mrs Platt curtsied (Father had insisted, it was traditional) or rather parodied a curtsy and went — where according to family lore it was rumoured she cohabitated with a Mr Platt, rarely seen and paid quite handsomely when one considered his free bed and board and his five-year issue of winter clothing and other necessities, like studded boots and wellingtons. He was reputed to be the maintenance man but the household, having no concrete evidence of his existence, ceased to believe in him long ago. From time to time there were reports of sightings by moonlight or in the flash of summer lightning, but all were discounted as imagination on the part of the person reporting the apparition. Ghost or human, there was little evidence that he ever worked or toiled — toil, which in the biblical sense implied sweat, he most certainly did not.

She paused before the door to the study and bit her lip and otherwise steeled herself for what lay ahead. She entered the room and from the old armchair beloved of her father, Mr Chuckleworth rose creakily and bow-backed and she found herself, to her amazement, confronted by a man possibly in his early eighties, frail in frame, a shrunken face clearly showing the underlying framework of bone and two protruding eyes of a light misty blue unbecomingly rimmed by thin strips of exposed flesh which outlined the eyes and brought them into even sharper relief.

To her further astonishment, Gertrude found herself deeply moved almost to tears at the sight of the old crock in clerical garb and by the fact that he had most likely made the visit to the house — a journey of some miles — on foot. There was no evidence of a pony and trap outside (she no longer knew if he still possessed one) and Horton had certainly not brought him by his hackney car or the entire household would have heard the motor screech to a halt outside the door, churning up the gravel of the drive so much it would need attention.

To her sorrow, Mr Chuckleworth straightened his back to a point where he could straighten it no further. It was some time since last she saw him — surely not so long ago as her father's funeral? His decrepitude was appalling and, she noted, his eyes had a sadness wisdom forbade her to question and though they sometimes twinkled he never smiled with them, baring his teeth instead in what he fondly believed was a warm and generous beam.

"Forgive me my dear," he said, his voice quivering, "for this unwarrented intrusion. . . . But I felt I had to take my leave of the mortal remains of dear David, by your kind permission of course, my dear." He waved a tattered prayer-book with its coloured silken markers. "I thought to say a few prayers and to perform the burial service quietly to myself, and if needs be . . . alone." He paused and his head jerked involuntarily, his mouth twitched with pain and he uttered a low cry of distress.

She suddenly realised the man was mortally ill.

"Mr Chuckleworth? . . . Whatever is the matter?" She dashed forward and took him by the arm, gently she thought, though he at first winced and then bared his teeth in a grotesque parody of a smile. She sat him back in the armchair and reaching for the nearest bellrope, pulled it.

"How did you get here Mr Chuckleworth?" she demanded harshly . . . all too aware of the fact that in the matter of David's death, as in all the affairs of those she loved, she acted with ruthless selfishness in her efforts to protect and spare them, never for once considering the desires or needs of others, and was therefore totally unequipped to deal with the affection of others for those she so protected, least of all when confronted so brutally as she now was by Mr Chuckleworth and his undeniable affection.

Mr Chuckleworth twisted his head, extending it as far as it could be extended, and then with a gulp, quickly retracted it. There was a twinkle in his eye which belied the occasion and the place.

"Promise me my dear . . . my few prayers in silence and I shall tell you without hesitation."

Mrs Platt knocked on the door. The knock registered distinctly in the background of her mind. She stared unbelievingly at the old man.

"You walked here?" she said . . . and tears rose in her eyes and she suffered an inner intense pain that one could love David and she and very likely he himself . . . be unaware of it. She bowed her head and tried to gain control of her emotions. "My prayers," said Mr Chuckleworth raising aloft his prayerbook and waving it as if signalling forward Christian forces on the very field of battle. "My prayers," he repeated as if claiming a trophy.

"Of course," said Gertrude. "You have them but only in silence."

Mr Chuckleworth nodded his head and appeared to weep. It could, she told herself doggedly, be fluid from his inflamed sockets. . . . "'Pon my word, I've won a battle I was fully convinced I had lost even before it was begun." He nodded his head of sparse silver hair. "Yes my dear, I walked here. I suffer the fate of all the aged in the care of their own . . . a surfeit of love and over-zealous care and attention based on the belief that because one is aged, one is of necessity, in one's dotage. I slipped away when they left me to sleep on the sun porch because the years advance and I know I should never have the opportunity of coming this way again, besides the overwhelming desire to take my leave of David in a befitting manner. They would have stopped me my dear you see, if they once suspected my intentions. But one thing I shall ask of my God if I gain His presence and that is that I be permitted to frequently visit in spirit the house, and all those in it, I have come to love dearly over the years I have spent in this town as His servant." He hesitated, and when he spoke it was with sadness. "You see my dear, it is the fate of those who wear the cloth to love those in their care with an affection, if not love, which is rarely suspected and seldom, if ever, reciprocated."

Gertrude wept for the second time that morning, briefly and without restraint. Mrs Platt knocked again on the door, this time rattily and impatiently. "Wait, damn you woman! Wait," she exclaimed through a clenched fist which she held to her mouth. She bit her finger in an effort at self control and turned aside and found herself confronted by the water-colour of David done by Mrs Chuckleworth, the vicar's wife, long dead and in life an even more insubstantial figure than Mother had been.

He was astonishingly beautiful. His beauty was not of the angelic kind which borders on the feminine and approaches the androgynous which so appeals to the older invert. From a finely boned and trusting face, two dark blue eyes met the gaze of the viewer with disconcerting honesty and a total lack of mistrust or hostility of any kind. His nose was fine though slightly hooked — he had broken it when boxing when still quite young. His lips were generous and slightly parted, showing part of his perfect teeth. His chin was firm and well set. He sported the beginnings of a moustache on his upper lip which lent him an air of arrogance he did in fact possess. His hair, once wheaten, had darkened somewhat and

was creased rigidly down the centre of his head into what was
possibly two equal parts. He was in officer's uniform and
wore the ribbon of the Victoria Cross discreetly to the left of
his left lapel. Incongruously, Mrs Chuckleworth had painted
him against a flowering cherry in full blossom and in the
distance the sunset sky was streaked with pale saffron.

Remarkably it worked. It was the one watercolour of a
few which evoked for her his eternal boyishness which was
tinged nevertheless with the solemnity youth can so startlingly
summon. None of the many photographs of him were as
evocative. None captured his sensual beauty which had at
first aroused her admiration and love and, in time, unbidden
lust. . . . She deeply regretted that no one had painted or
photographed him in the nude, capturing permanently the
fawn-like beauty of his fine, white body. If only his injuries
had proved immediately fatal, she thought bitterly, remem-
bering the long, embittering years since then and now. The
task which confronted her later in the morning was salt to
what was already a gaping wound.

Mrs Platt knocked on the door again, this time with a firm-
ness which bordered on the impertinent.

"Come in woman," she exclaimed, aware of the black
hatred on her face, the serpentine hiss in her voice, the black-
clothed dereliction which was the vicar ensconced in Father's
chair. Ignoring the presence of Mrs Platt behind her she
addressed him directly. "You could perhaps do with some
tea, vicar, after your long journey on foot. And perhaps some
honey and toast to refuel you for the return journey. You do
need something," she added with unwarranted malice "at
your age."

Mr Chuckleworth again stretched his neck to its limit,
swallowing a handsome morsel in one bit, and then, after
retracting his neck and striking himself rather penitentially on
the chest, he said, "Yes my dear, I do believe I will have
something. I further agree that indeed I do need something at
my age. But," he added rising with difficulty from the depths
of the chair, "only after my prayers."

Gertrude addressed Mrs Platt without turning to face her.
"Some tea and toast for the vicar, Mrs Platt. Here in the
study please. And . . . " she added, venemously, noting from

her shadow that Mrs Platt had failed to curtsy on entering the room, "you have been with this family long enough to know how to correctly enter and leave a room when bidden."

She turned to face Mrs Platt who flushed the deepest red and then paled as though all blood had drained from her body. She curtsied and muttered, "Yes, Madam . . . I beg your pardon, Madam," and withdrew closing the door behind her with infinite care as she left the room. Mr Chuckleworth beamed at her in what he thought was jolly good Christian fellowship. Mrs Platt shot him a glance as though he had spat at her. They heard her retreat down the passage towards the kitchen. The kitchen door was flung open and then banged shut in savage fury. Over the years Mrs Platt had made the door the one instrument by which and through which she expressed her true feelings to her husband and, less directly, to the rest of the household, without as a convention, any risk of censure.

"That," muttered Gertrude savagely, "will have to be stopped."

"Pardon my dear," said Mr Chuckleworth believing it was he who was addressed.

"Nothing vicar. I was talking to myself. Anno Domini and all that."

Mr Chuckleworth shook his head and cackled, "Oh, I know all about that! I do so indeed . . . oh dear me yes!"

Gertrude felt any good will and compassion aroused by the vicar's visit, his decrepitude and the fact that he had arrived on foot, was fast ebbing away. "Much more of this torment and I shall scream. I'll wreak havoc on the nearest human being be he or she as white as the legendary driven snow, or the lamb of purest innocence."

"I'll take you to David's room Mr Chuckleworth but please," she added, feeling her heart harden and her voice take on a bitter edge not wholly warranted, "no prayers or intonations aloud. You may pray to your heart's desire, but not aloud."

"Of course my dear, I understand," said Mr Chuckleworth, following her from the room.

Oh no you don't, my fine, feathered friend, she thought, you don't know. You don't know at all. And not if you lived for a million years could you possibly be expected to begin to understand. No one could, she thought bitterly . . . not even Anna. Anna, whom she loved greatly and who loved her deeply in return . . . kind, beaten, broken-backed Anna who like a brutally treated hound, possibly much kicked, responded to love or affection at its simplest, with a fullness and openness of the heart which so frightened her, its recipient, to such an extent she almost felt compelled to say, "Dear God, don't love me so much, so deeply, so simply . . . the loving heart leaves itself open to betrayals of all kind, not least the treason of another human heart."

"I do hope, vicar, the stairs won't prove too much for you." And no sooner had she said it than she realised he was having the greatest difficulty in climbing the stairs and none but a simpleton would have failed to foresee as much. He was, she saw, experiencing not just difficulty but, visibly, pain. For one fleeting moment she wondered if that was unconsciously why she had agreed to allow him to see David in death. If so, she found herself relenting completely and proffered her arm as support which was gratefully accepted. Together they climbed the stairs in silence and she found herself thinking of the old man by her side as being nothing but skin and bone . . . nothing at all. His bones like those of a bird, hollow, brittle and breakable . . . burnable. Skin and bone, his once-striking form now greatly reduced, like David's.

They entered the darkened room and Mr Chuckleworth stood uncertainly inside the door trying to adjust his eyes to the almost total absence of light. "Just a moment vicar," she said, "I'll pull the curtains further. I keep them drawn as a protection against the sunlight though we hardly get any here at all except when the earth is in its summer orbit. Sunlight hurt his eyes so we hardly ever exposed them to the full light of day." Her voice trailed off and she was aware of the waves of shock assaulting the body of Mr Chuckleworth like a storm-driven sea assaulting in wave after wave a smooth, innocent beach. Yes, she thought, it was stupid of me. He hasn't seen David for years. He most likely remembers him as he was as a youth. The corpse on the bed would, she realised, be judged by the average person unaware of the facts, as of a

man in his late sixties. It was not the body of a young man so
freely gifted by nature in both body and mind — the kind
which was so prevalent before the Great War — the kind they
now snidely refer to as 'golden'.

Mr Chuckleworth steadied himself and fumbled with his
prayer-book and began his intonation of prayer and bene-
diction. Characteristically for one so old, he thought himself
as praying silently. His voice rose and fell in the quiet, warm
room like a bee buzzing from blossom to blossom in a field
of clover.

How very simply it had all begun. The night warm, the faint-
est breeze blowing with cooling effect over her sleeping form.
She had been sleeping deeply. The deep sleep with which the
young anticipate sun-drenched days and a hundred trifling
things to do, none of which were of any real importance what-
ever but which in retrospect added to the total one considered
the carefree days of youth so carelessly squandered.

He tapped lightly on her door and entered quietly calling,
"Bunch, Bunch, are you awake?" His voice was soft and
excited and she knew he had some adventure in mind.
"Bunch, Bunch," he called again, his voice taking on a
greater urgency, a sense of plea which was David at his most
winning self.

"What is it?" she growled, turning over, enveloped by the
luxury of bodily warmth and deep, dreamless sleep. She open-
ed her eyes and looked at him. The night was quiet and
tranquil, the stars visible with diamond clarity and in the
middle distance the sea murmured softly. A pale silver light
less than moonlight lit the room. He was clad only in shorts
and a white shirt and a pair of white tennis shoes and white
socks which were his summer wear and which he sported
whatever the weather and whatever the circumstances. He
had only one set of clothing and each night washed every-
thing, shirts, shorts, underpants and socks, and whitened the
tennis shoes before drying everything in the boiler room for
use the next morning. She knew of old he always slept naked
between a pair of sheets and covered only by one virtually
threadbare blanket which was a relic of the nursery.

He smelt of outdoor freshness. He was splendidly develop-
ed. It was his first year at Cambridge and she had been afraid
that he would change so much . . . Become self-conscious and
fall prey to affectations of one kind or another, just to show
how adult and independent he had become. But he hadn't
changed at all. First day back on vacation he had raised
murder when he found his bed properly made up as it should
be. He stripped it in an impressive rage and spent the night
wrapped in a blanket in an easy chair having bundled out all
the bedclothes and ordered a search for his old, rather tatty
blanket. It was eventually discovered being used as under-
covering for a litter of kittens Mrs Platt was fostering in the
kitchen. When mother had informed him of the fact and
reasonably suggested that he settle for another blanket, he
had looked at her quizzically and with startling simplicity he
had insisted that the blanket be taken from the kittens, boiled
thoroughly twice over and exchanged for the blanket he had
been sleeping on. Mother had consented with that soft sigh
which marked her slow descent into that state of quiet
despair which seemed her ordained state of being.

"What is it?" she demanded irritably, yet so glad in her
heart he had come. He sat on her bed and ruffled her hair
and without the slightest hesitation he slipped a hand inside
her nightdress and fondled her breasts which were very nearly
at their fullest and finest. He kissed her lightly on the cheek
and then, at her insistence, less lightly on the lips and she
wondered why, since they had taken to kissing in so direct
a manner some years before, his mouth tasted of the white
flesh of the apple and tasted somewhat like cider or a light,
bitter-sweet wine. She reached out and touched his broad
thighs and he laughed and ruffled her hair again and said,
"Come on Bunch, come on out for a swim. It's simply
terrific on the strand. I've been there already and I thought
how wonderful it all is. . . . Bunch should be here with
me. . . . Dash it all Bunch. . . . Come along, all you need is
a blanket around your shoulders. No shoes. . . nothing else
whatever."

And she had gone and found that he had lit a fire in a
hollow in the sand-dunes and had brought the metal tri-
pod Father had made for them in the days when they used

to hike long distances and sometimes, as a very special treat, sleep under canvas for the night. From it hung their old billycan. She could see the neat tin box which contained tea and sugar and salt and had tiny corked bottles for mustard and other seasonings which they took on their hikes or picnics on the beach in the long summer evenings, though it was understood they had to be home by ten o'clock at the latest. Their illicit picnics which were far more adventuresome, took part in the very early hours of the mornings and lasted until dawn coloured the sky and there was a reverent hush over both sea and land preparatory to sunrise.

"Sly-boots," she taunted on seeing the carefully made preparations.

And he laughed so lovingly and gracefully and without ceremony of any kind stripped naked and stood still while she examined his superb body in detail, her eyes lingering over his thighs and the evidence of his advancing manhood. "Come on Bunch, old thing," he said, "don't keep me waiting." Shyly she slipped the blanket from about her shoulders and loosening her nightdress, she allowed it to slip down about her feet and stepped lightly out of it, feeling the fresh, moist morning air which had an invigorating sting to it. And he murmured, "My God Bunch, you're the beauty of them all." He caught her roughly and held her body tightly to his while he played up and down her bare back and buttocks and his thighs thrust rhythmically and arousingly at hers. And, just when she was beginning to respond he broke from her and shouting, "Last one in is a dodo," he dashed the short distance to the sea and running through the shallows, he struck deep waters and plunged forward and disappeared under, holding his breath to see if he could stay there longer than three minutes, the length it was reputed to take a man to drown. And she watched nervously knowing with all her heart and soul nothing whatever would happen to him. In all that he dared to do, David was invulnerable, indestructible, a law unto himself. And then he burst to the surface spluttering and splattering, his body streaming water, sparkling in the night light.

With a hoarse war cry, she dashed forward and met him

and they thrashed about and shouted and tried to outswim or outdive each other for hours on end, until spent and exhausted and somewhat debilitated, they left the water. He hand-dried her body and in turn his own and draped the blanket about her shoulders while he sat on a towel or simply squatted while blowing life into the dying embers of the fire and his genitals swung freely, clearly visible, and she was irresistibly drawn to them and she loved him for the innocence with which he displayed them knowing how they attracted her. He allowed her to satisfy the hunger of her eyes while pretending to be oblivious of her attentions. In turn she noted gratefully that he was not unaware of her developing body and on a few occasions she had seen signs of sexual arousal which he sought to hide and failing to do so, insisted on another dip or excused himself mumbling something about the call of nature.

They drank strong tea pleasantly tasting of wood and ate avariciously sandwiches or whatever food David could manage to grab when he raided Mrs Platt's pantry. Then that night when the sea glistened with starlight and there were phosphorescent spreads on the water, he laid out the blanket and pulled her gently down and lay on her and expertly excited her to a pitch where she could no longer refuse him, not wholly because of his excitement but because of the sexual hunger which was rife in her lower body. She wept and laughed and then, utterly spent, wept again and he said, his brow furrowed, his eyes anxious as he asked, "Did I hurt you old thing?" and she said "Yes." He had hurt her but the pain was part of it all and then, still perplexed, he asked, knowing that he had deflowered her, "You don't think I'm rotten or anything like that. . . . I mean, you don't feel despoiled or cheapened or anything like that?" And she said, "No, you stupid goose, of course not. . . quite the opposite if anything," and they had coupled again with even greater abandonment than before and with the light of dawn streaking across the eastern sky, they had returned quietly to the house, slipped inside, kissed quickly and then parted each to their own rooms, hearing as they did so Mrs Platt beginning to stoke the kitchen stove and begin her day of grim service amongst the pots and pans,

steam and heat. Mrs Platt knew all about them. David told
her she knew with stunning bluntness at the end of the
holidays but Mrs Platt never showed the slightest sign of
knowing or caring. Mother, she sensed, knew. Her large
blue eyes, which were her gift of the blood to David, were
as always, soft and luminescent, full as ever with love and not
a little sadness and her mouth which was big and unbeauti-
fully shaped with her unfortunate teeth, which were not of
uniform length — she knew. She knew but if she cared she
kept it as she kept all things, secret, hidden in the recesses
of her mind to which she alone had access when in the early
hours of the morning and her torment was at its utmost, she
did indeed examine them in detail and inevitably lapsed into
deep despair and did sad, silly things like cropping her beauti-
ful hair and tearing tufts of it from her head, leaving her bald
and bleeding in spots and the rest ragged and uneven, like the
coat of a ill-fed mongrel, or more seriously, disfiguring her
face and her very beautiful hands with razor blades. The
times when she had to go or to be taken to what she called
softly "that place" for months on end, very often for more
than a year and where in fact she died. Possibly, just possibly,
Mother, who suffered so much, was human enough, substantial
enough, to care. If only a little.

Mr Chuckleworth finished his incantations which she found
were not without beauty and possibly with the power to
sooth and heal if one could believe. She knew she could not
and their falsity struck as much as did their lyrical beauty
and the intensity of Mr Chuckleworth's delivery. Sunstruck
he stood by the bed and then, as if revitalised from an inner
source, he raised his right hand in benediction and pro-
nounced the blessing as if confronted by the entire congre-
gation of St James's.
    "The peace of Almighty God descend upon you dear
David, through Our Lord Jesus Christ. . . and remain with
you for ever. Amen."
    And, bending with great dignity, he gently kissed the face
of the shrunken form on the bed and, in passing, very gently
the sparse white hair which once was lush and wheaten.

She felt angered when first she saw him bend to kiss David. She thought irrationally that he was about to perpetrate some unspeakable outrage which would greatly lessen David already greatly lessened in death as he had been in life. But when she saw the gentle kiss, the touching of the hair, she cried out in distress and then quickly stifled the cry.

Mr Chuckleworth tottered toward her. "And you too my dear." He kissed her not once but thrice, once on each cheek in the continental manner and then once on the forehead. "Goodbye my dear. You are no stranger to grief and sorrow and other outrages. May God bless you with tranquility and peace of mind and. . .," he hesitated, "perhaps a little happiness in what remains of your life." She thanked him and felt that his kindness, his quite unexpected kindness, had been like so many body blows. Had he resorted to sactimonious banalities she could have savaged him with all the pent-up fury she harboured at David's death. Undone and feeling totally spent emotionally, she led him downstairs to the study to where breakfast awaited him on the small table before the chair where Father had loved to dine alone, no matter how many of the family were home, or how many guests there might be. Mr Chuckleworth took refuge in the chair like a tortoise taking shelter in his shell, murmuring, "My, my, my, what a positive treat," at what was only well-buttered toast lightly done, an egg hard-boiled, tea in a small china teapot and a jar of commercial honey. She left him to eat in peace. There was no difficulty whatever in withdrawing. After the first bite of toast liberally spread with honey he was oblivious of her presence. Glancing back she saw him take his pocket watch from the pocket in his waistcoat and, flicking it neatly open, lay it carefully on the table by him. He took the jar of honey in his hand and glanced at it endearingly. "My, my," he softly exclaimed, "Do they still make that?"

No sooner had she entered the hall and closed the study door behind her than she heard what she had been dreading all morning. The crunch of the wheels of a smoothly moving motor on the gravel of the drive outside and the appearance of the black bonnet of the hearse visible through the tinted glass of the porch window as it drew up almost noiselessly outside the hall door.

Just then, Anna came downstairs dressed in restrained elegance, all in black, a small purse tucked under her arm, her veil thrown back over her head and lying about her head like the elaborately folded veils with which Renaissance men loved to enfold the exquisite faces of their Madonnas.

"They're here," said Gertrude and suddenly she felt sick and very frightened. She paled visibly.

Anna took her by the hand. "You had better come with me. What you need is a cup of tea and something to eat. You haven't eaten for days." And shrugging aside all resistance, she steered her towards the small, sunlit room which served as a breakfast-room in winter where it caught more sunlight than did the actual dining-room.

It consisted simply of a dining table, a number of chairs arranged at spaced intervals around the table, each appearing jealous of their particular position and fearing encroachment from one or other of the rooms flanking it. They had plush seat padding and plush padded backing. Blue, faded to an almost grey hue. The oval carpet which was threadbare had likewise fallen victim to the sunlight over the years and though barely discernible, one could see blue had featured at one time in the colouring. The walls were papered a pale blue and they too seemed more grey than blue. The windows had no curtains and were shuttered if at all necessary.

In a corner stood a lacquered screen they had never dared claim as being genuinely Chinese, but which was nevertheless a first-class example of workmanship. They described it in what was a family joke, not altogether without pride, as being from the Tinshu period. Nobody had ever questioned the description. It was black with a perfect mixture of the deepest orange and crimson and its greatest glory, the subdued use of gold and green and blue. It depicted a rampaging dragon against a forest of flames while further flames issued from its mouth and nostrils.

It was, she remembered, as Anna shepherded her to a chair and saw her seated before going to fetch some food and to take care of the undertakers, initially at least — the same screen which father had moved to his study when he was ill and behind which he retreated whenever he had to use the kidney-shaped enamel bowl to relieve himself of the blaubs of blood and other mucus which forced its way to his mouth from his diseased stomach. She had, she remembered, quite deliberately waited until he was sleeping deeply in front of the fire in the chair now occupied by Mr Chuckleworth, and trespassed carefully and cautiously — and in retrospect with what she had to admit was appalling callousness — behind the screen and it had given her such a malignant glee to see the basin laid in the centre of the table and flanked by a pile of neatly folded hand towels and a carafe of water with a small tumbler by its side. They were all set out on a bamboo table draped with a linen tablecloth, harshly white, and its folds showing clearly and it struck her that her father had entered into the worship of a god of his own and was involved in the almost sacramental act of dying — slowly and painfully. Of cancer of the stomach. He knew as much and hated the fact and what was more, loathed her because he had charged he had been severed from her and hence from life with what was tantamount to biblical ruthlessness. She realised and the doctor had confirmed her belief that father had undergone a personality change due to his illness, and he, the most genial of men, had become ugly minded, spiteful and vindictive, suffering greatly, dying slowly and loving only David with a fidelity which was touching. He did not remain faithful to his new god to the death. He shot himself in the head late one night in his study behind this very screen and so spared himself great pain and her a great deal of misery though that, she believed, had not been his prime intention. Now she stared dully at the screen, seeing and not seeing, remembering in great detail while she waited for Anna and whatever food Anna would bring her. Suddenly she experienced the need for a cigarette with the sharp assertive need of a heavy smoker. She smoked rarely but nevertheless carried a packet with her. In company she found it gave her something to do and distracted from her otherwise restless hands. She fumbled in her neatly tailored costume coat. There were none there. Swiftly and unthinkingly she dashed out and into the kitchen. Seeing Mrs Platt wasn't there, she rummaged about in the lower half of a dresser where she knew Mrs Platt

kept hers in her purse. There was a packet there together
with Mrs Platt's Post Office savings book, some opened
letters, a few photographs and some money. She knew what
the contents of the bag were likely to be. When children,
she and David periodically raided the kitchen and indeed the
bedrooms of the other servants when they had other servants,
and examined their private belongings in great detail. They
did so with glee and somehow it gave a malicious delight,
a certain power in fact, to know what was essentially none of
their business. Servants, they concluded, were not entitled
to the privilege of privacy as they were not entitled to other
things. She took the packet of cigarettes from the purse and
slung the purse carelessly on the table where some of the
contents spilled out. Gratefully she took a cigarette from the
packet, lit it and inhaled deeply. She felt the smoke curl
comfortingly about in her lungs and then thought, whatever
will Mrs Platt think? And aloud, answered her own question,
"Blast Mrs Platt," and leaving the handbag on the table she
returned to the breakfast-room clutching the packet of
cigarettes and a box of matches. If the bitch comes near
me, she swore silently, I'll reef the two eyes out of her bloody
head, and took her place at the table once more having found
an ashtray on the mantlepiece.

The village clock chimed and, Gertrude thought, it's
all a matter of hours and there'll hardly be anything to live
for anymore. Anna, perhaps, but then in a way she found
difficult to define even to her own satisfaction, there were
limits to her affections and her love for Anna. She loved her,
yes. . . very much so, but to what extent and in what measure
was something which time alone could determine and define.
It was really a question of which was the greater love, and
just now there could be no doubt about the question. Her
love for David was overwhelmingly to the fore and had been
in all her relationships with Anna. How, she pondered, could
Anna ever be expected to realise that? How could she ever
understand what could not and would not be ever explained
to her? The true nature of her love for David, its depths, its
physical realities at least in the past. And above all how in-
separably he was a part of her. So much so that she felt a
huge chunk of consciousness had been torn from her mind,

and her body in some way had been detruncated or so
greatly and painfully lessened that she was astonished to see
herself reflected in a mirror or any reflecting surface as whole
and entire while she suffered physically like one having sus-
tained greater bodily injury. She heard footsteps and suddenly
felt guilty about swiping Mrs Platt's cigarettes and matches
and prepared to defend herself against charges of invasion of
the woman's privacy if not indeed outright trespass which
she vaguely realised was not without certain legal compli-
cations. But then she remembered that Mrs Platt moved like
a vapour, much as Mother had done. Her arrivals and depar-
tures were more a matter of apparition than of movement
from one place to another. It could only be Anna.

The door opened and with difficulty she edged a break-
fast tray through the doorway and laid it on the table before
her. On it was as substantial a meal as she had laid before
Anna herself some time ago. She stared at the food and
thought stupidly... when I entered the kitchen to fetch
some cigarettes... there was no one there and no sign of
cooking.

My God, she thought, I'm going stark, raving mad. In a
few seconds my mind will snap like a metal hoop about a
barrel snapping under continual stress or through constric-
tion during a period of intense cold. People didn't realise
metal was subjected to such stresses and behaved like that.
But it did. And so did humans. They went mad. Stark,
raving mad, suddenly and without any prior warning what-
ever.

Her instinct was to vomit there and then, without cere-
mony or civility of any kind.

"Eat a little," Anna said in her gentle voice which still
retained the waif-like sorrow which was so striking a feature
of her voice when first she had heard her speak some five
years before when she had gone to the train to meet her.
She went expecting a rather verminous, snotty brat bearing
all the marks of bad nutrition and because she knew she
was a refugee and had been previously lodged with a Jewish
family, she had expected someone with what Father termed
the 'Shylock streak' about her. In simpler and less likeable
terms that meant something of the mean, the vicious and

the ruthless, not to speak of sly calculation and a willingness to plunder when possible. Not of course that Father was anti-Semitic. Oh no. . . not at all! But he did have connections with the City and indeed carried out a fair deal of transactions there and had a rather snide contempt about what he termed "the brotherhood of the hooked nose" and when you really looked at things pragmatically and un-emotionally, Mosley was a very, very intelligent man and a lot of what he said made sense. . . . And instead of a vermin-ridden brat who wasn't even house-trained, she was confront-ed by Anna, her Anna, her long, black hair glistening and which she thought seemed touched with green or the silver-purple of a sloe in early morning sunlight. Her eyes, large and luminous, deeply, wonderfully so, mirroring truth-fully her reactions to all events as did the sky, the changes of wind and temperature. Dressed neatly. All in school-girl grey and carrying her gas mask in its box and the smallest suitcase imaginable and offering her as a gift a conch shell which seemed too big for her to carry and which she clearly feared she would let fall and break. "Shell, sea shell," she murmured and then wept and they embraced and knew for the first time the warmth of each other's body and, inexplicably, both knew the true nature of their sexuality and, word unspoken, they both silently swore never to seek to deny or conceal it.

And with something akin to joy, she carried home her refugee who could hardly speak any proper English but proved a superb and willing pupil . . . home to 'Scanton' where her father had shot himself and David lay in drug-induced ecstasy and contentment in a world totally removed from theirs. . . so removed that all he had in common with the living was the fact he too would die one day. And the daily task of attending to David's bodily needs. . . what she thought of as his carcass, thin and feeble, bore little resem-blance to the fawn-like beauty of his youth — brought thoughts of murder to mind and she longed to press with just a little pressure about his throat and end his misery and hers. But his eyes, his eyes above all she loved about him bodily or spiritually, his eyes were treasurable and mirrored the inner sadness and the sheer anguish of existence. They mirrored also the happiness induced by the regulated doses of drugs needed to offset the slow but unalterable decay of his central nervous system and which held him captive and yet alone, of any substance on the face of the earth allowed him to live. Misted, his eyes glinting dimly, he appeared to sail on and on and on, interiorly journeying forever towards that spot, that tiny pin-point beyond the most distant of known and unknown galaxies, possibly beyond infinity itself, to where all that were one and whole and were broken, will be made one and whole again and he would laugh, his eyes intensely bright with sexual playfulness and he would hiss teasingly, "Let's kiss Bunch. . . let's kiss." But wherever that point might be and whenever he might be revitalised again, she could never hope to be there nor could any other living being.

His voice, black, bitter, bilious, all so uncharacteristically so, his tears flowing freely, murmuring brokenly in the days when he was less distant than he had been for many years back. "They broke me, Bunch old thing. . . . Don't you see that?. . . They broke my back, my spirit, my psyche, my soul. . . call it what you will. This trifle, this, this vaunted piece of metal inscribed 'For Valour' was awarded to me for the act of total folly in my life. You see I saw a fellow I knew to see. Not in my own command. . . go up and over and something made me stop and watch with the greatest curiosity. I remember thinking he doesn't stand an earthly. He's for it, for sure. And then I thought he's just a dolt, a mutton-headed yokel with no imagination, lacking most if not all the finer sensibilities. . . which as far as I was concerned, placed him a little, just a little, above the shittened beasts of the field. The pale moon of morning was visible coexistent with the risen sun and the grey, misty light touched him and I remembered how I had watched him surreptitiously for days, admiring his crude beauty and, God, I loved him and all he stood for, because I knew he was of the world and of worldly things like fruit and flowers and animals and of men and women and children and of his family and the land of his birth. . . a true and worthy inheritor of his forefathers. I knew he was what we, his so-called superiors, intellectualised ourselves to be. He was living, intensely, vibrantly and brilliantly. As ready to live and shine like some major star of the heavens or a small insignificant planet destined to shine dimly and then fall darkly into the dark void of death. He was prepared to be what fate ordained him to be and he never questioned his lot for one second. I saw him struck and virtually obliterated before my very eyes and I thought of him and the splendour of his body — and believe me Bunch, he was above all splendid — and I thought the stupid, asinine fools, our military superiors, are sending tens of thousands, perhaps not quite as splendid as you, but splendid never-theless, out to certain, senseless slaughter with no bloody right whatever. And I thought as I saw him fall clutching his bursted face. . . I'll see you die decently, in my arms if possible. . . . I'll see you lie in a grave and not just ploughed or churned into the mud like thousands of others I've seen. . . and so I ran and caught him as he fell and saw the full stupe-fication in his eyes as he died. . . . And I thought. . . the fool. . . the utter, stupid fool never realised that he was alive until just then and I held him as tightly as I could and wept and wept and suddenly I saw a movement to my left and saw someone sling a hand grenade and I just watched it drop and then quite unthinkingly I picked it up and slung it back and saw three men in a machine-gun nest splay out like fractured dolls. They were blown to bits within yards of me. . . . Their gun must have jammed. . . and they smelt foul. You don't know how foul smelling humans are under their skein of skin. . . and then again without any conscious thought I ran to the gun and kicked it savagely in frustration and turned it on the Jerries, who were advancing to capture the lost outpost. Miraculously it worked and I gunned them like lifeless targets at a rifle-range. I waved my men forward and they advanced in great spirit and we took an enclave which had jutted into our territory and which in the past had cost us dearly in human life. For that. . . sham — because that was all it was — they gave us this, the V.C., but they knew it was all a sham. You see I kissed him as he died and nothing was ever as delightful or sweeter or as lovable, and with his dying breath and his last expenditure of strength he could muster, he returned my kiss. . . fully and without qualification. And that's what makes it so very bloody. Had he laughed or scorned or spat or even bit me, I could have coped. I could have covered up. But he didn't. He kissed me with the terrible passion of the dying and then died and slid to the muddy earth at my feet and I thought, my fine and splendid fellow, the one and only Alexander of my age — you deserved more than this. . . much, much more than this. More than all the world could be made to give to you and your kind who gave life so lightly for the imperial dreams of others. But you never had it and you never will. They'll see to that. . . So you see, they broke me Bunch, they broke me. . . as calculatingly as someone picking a growing reed and breaking it. . . and you remember what mother used to murmur when she was ill and suffering at her most internally, in there beyond her sad and lovely eyes. . . . "Broken reeds can never be repaired nor shattered minds be made whole. . . . I'm like that. I'm just like that, Bunch old thing. They gave me this decoration 'For Valour' and then they tried to persuade me to travel around the country on a recruiting campaign. . . . Marching men and blaring bands. . . . Platforms draped with Union Jacks and the national flags of Our Glorious Allies. . . and lots of bunting and the local nobility or what passes locally for nobility. And me, of course, the prize exhibit. The hero who faced the mortal enemy and virtually engaged him in single-handed combat, smiling modestly while someone sang my praises and then I would rise to spew all their stupid filth about patriotism and the war being fought to save civilisation. They wanted me, in short, to be a Judas goat — to lead others, hundreds, thousands, if possible, into the senseless slaughter I had witnessed for weeks on end until I virtually ceased to think of the fellows as human beings. They wanted me to send as many as possible to die the death *he* died in the ankle-deep mud on a pale, misty morning. I refused. . . I refused point blank. So they accused me of cowardice, amongst other things. You see, there had been others, less fleeting, more intimate and yet infinitely less memorable than he. Some officers had witnessed the last scene from a distance of some miles. Through dust and dirt and shells exploding the bastards saw and recorded what they had seen and then they tried to skewer me on the fact and rumours of past

behaviour. I still refused. Then I was summoned to see one of
the big bods at G.H.Q. He told me that if I refused to co-
operate I would die as certainly as if by execution. He per-
sonally would see that time after time and against all
regulations to the contrary, I would be sent over the top
until I was fatally injured. My death, he assured me, would
be hailed in the newspapers of virtually every capital in the
English-speaking world as the ultimate sacrifice of a sterling
hero. "I'll see you die," he said. "Gloriously or ignominiously.
It doesn't really matter how. . . but die you shall. . . and be
hailed." He was wrong, Bunch old thing. Mathematically I
should be dead. Statistically I may be said to be dead. In
reality I'm nothing but a broken body and a broken mind. . . .
They've had their way. They broke me. They sent me to my
death. I can't begin to describe the pain I suffer. The physi-
cal pain I can tolerate. . . it's the metal anguish which maims
most. I keep seeing him Bunch as I saw him that morning as
he took a cheap cigarette from his lips and ground it under-
foot and licked his lips nervously before going over the top.
And what happened, happened, and I know in my heart of
hearts that I'd do it all again. You understand, Bunch old
thing. . . you understand? You don't mind me raving on and
on like this? You see I can't help it. They done me in, quite
deliberately, and I have to exist as I am. You do under-
stand, don't you?"

And she said, "Yes, I understand." But no, she never had.
Not until now.

Anna placed her face to hers and pressed against her stroking
with her left hand the hair on the other side of her head.
She took a scented handkerchief and dried her tears and said
with strange, uncharacteristic authority, "Eat. Just a little.
Then we can both do what must be done."

Anna's eyes were appealing in a way which brooked no
refusal. She ate a little toast, or rather nibbled a little, and
thought of Mr Chuckleworth ensconced in Father's chair
in the study and how amusing she had thought he had looked
nibbling furtively like a mouse not wholly trusting its good
fortune in finding a complete slice of bread. She attempted

something more substantial but her stomach rebelled. She pushed the food from her.

"Good. Even a little is better than nothing," Anna said in sombre, solemn tones and wafted away the plate of bacon and sausages and the toast but leaving the pot of tea, milk and sugar. After Anna had gone she took another cigarette from Mrs Platt's packet and again lit one and inhaled deeply with intense, demeaning hunger. There was a sharp, short tap on the door. The tap of a total stranger. She looked up in surprise and not without anger.

"Who is it?" she called out and heard a man reply in funeral tones. "It is I, Madam." Stupid, she thought. Grammatically correct but hardly revealing or informative. "Do come in," she called out in an iced, polite voice, stubbing her cigarette out in the ashtray in front of her and assuming quite unconsciously the superior attitude without which it was impossible to deal with underlings, and stood to meet the possessor of the deep voice. She was not surprised to find the door open slowly and a man dressed all in black, impeccable in appearance and with the carefully acquired manners of one she imagined to be a mandarin or an official at the court of a mandarin.

"What is it please?" she enquired with defensive harshness, knowing exactly what it was that brought him while at the same time a tiny, inner voice tinged with hysteria asked how many mandarins had she met or how many officials of a mandarin's court had she known. She suppressed the urge to laugh shrilly and inappropriately as the humour of the question struck her. The man in black with the cool, deep eyes of a detached professional showed no involvement with the human aspect of his profession and when he spoke he spoke without adopting the odiously false tone of bereavement one might expect of him. He bowed slightly and said in a clear, precise voice, "Madam, we are expected at the crematorium at eleven a.m. As it is we can't possibly make it now. . . but if we are too late we will miss our appointment altogether and will have to wait until last."

She hadn't thought there'd be many. . . a few perhaps, but hardly as many as the man implied.

"Are there many then?. . . I mean for this morning?"

"A considerable number Madam, for the entire day. We would appreciate it if you would supervise the coffining of the remains."

Her stomach churned at the use of the word 'remains' which she knew was the true and accurate description of what lay in the bed in David's bedroom. Her head seemed to swivel about from an area of bright, white light to one of dense, threatening darkness. Vaguely her mind registered the tinkle of the bell on the back door in the kitchen and she realised that Mrs Platt had returned. She summoned what strength she could and straightened herself and replied in a voice which struck herself by its firmness. "I'll supervise matters. Please come with me," and taking each step knowing each one brought her closer to the total realisation of David's death, she started across the room towards the door which led to the hall. The man in black stood back and inclined his upper-body fractionally. She heard rapid footsteps on the hard, polished linoleum of the hall, then the door to the room was thrown open and Mrs Platt entered the room, her face black with rage. Throwing aside the man in black — had he introduced himself? She'd forgotten — and holding high her empty handbag she demanded sharply, "Did you do this Madam?" Her voice was steady and steel hard, her lower lip and the area immediately below pulled down the tension distorting all her features and baring her lower teeth and portions of her very pink gums. "Well yes," she began, trying to explain as reasonably as possible what she had done and why she had done it, when Mrs Platt repeated her question and she admitted she had emptied the bag. Eyes blazing with fury Mrs Platt demanded, "Why?"

"Because," she said coldly, angered by the woman's mutinous behaviour, "I needed a cigarette."

Mrs Platt's face blackened further, her rage intensified. She shouted rather than spoke, her voice rising eventually to what was virtually a naked scream. "*You* needed a cigarette and so *you* went and ferretted out my handbag containing all my private papers and valuables like a common thief and then like a dirty slut you throw everything about the kitchen table and without as much as 'May I or By-your-leave' you *stole* my cigarettes!"

"Stole?" she replied, reeling under the onslaught. "There was no question of stealing anything Mrs Platt. I merely borrowed a few cigarettes." She laughed lightly, unconvincingly. "Really Mrs Platt, surely you exaggerate. I admit it was tactless of me not to ask you first but at the time you were nowhere to be found and I. . . ."

"You stole one from my handbag. You hear me? . . . stole! That's the proper word Madam. . . stole. Not borrowed or anything else but stole. . . . " The angry woman drew breath. "Well Madam, let me tell you something. Like it or not, there's a law against that sort of thing in this country. Theft of private property it's called."

"Really Mrs Platt, you forget yourself. Remember who you are and where you are."

"I haven't forgotten for one moment who I am or where I am."

"My brother is upstairs. . . ."

Triumph shone in Mrs Platt's eyes. Instinctively Gertrude knew she was mistaken in ever mentioning David.

"I know Madam. . . . I know your brother is upstairs. The dirty bastard is dead at last. You hear me? He was nothing more than a downright, dirty bastard!"

She struck out with her fist. Mrs Platt swayed and then fell against the man in black who, like Anna in the doorway, was staring with astonishment at the pair of them. Blood trickled freely from Mrs Platt's nose. Now the triumph in her eyes was even greater and more malignant. She allowed herself to be helped to her feet by the man in black, staunching the alarming flow of blood from her nose with her right hand.

"That's assault Madam," she said in deadly venom which was hard and compact as if stored with care over a number of years. . . decades possibly. "That's assault and battery," she continued in her distorted voice. "There's a law against that Madam. Like there is against theft and trespass." She turned to go.

"Mrs Platt, really! Come here please and let me attend to your nose."

"Don't touch me you filthy bitch. . . . As if I didn't know what went on for years with that bugger upstairs. . . . And now you have that other filthy little bitch to play about with. . . .

Touch me with as much as one of your little fingers and I'll tear the face off you, you filthy pervert. And neither judge nor jury would find me guilty."

She reeled. She saw Anna turn aside as though lanced in the side, pain diluting the bright glimmer of her care and affection. The man in black stared in frank fascination, looking from one speaker to another as though witnessing a first-rate drama for which he had duly paid his admittance fee. Her voice came from afar. "You're dismissed Mrs Platt. As and from now. I'll take care of things when I return."

Mrs Platt leered at her and then coldly and very deliberately she spat in her face and waited for retaliation. There was none and turning on her heels she left the room, her feet beating defiantly on the linoleum of the hall. The kitchen door was banged shut with insolent loudness.

The man in black coughed uncomfortably. Anna dashed forward and was about to wipe the spittle from her face.

"Please Anna. Don't touch me. Not now."

Anna, stung — withdrew.

Carefully she took a handkerchief from her jacket pocket and wiped her face, not altogether oblivious of the dejection in Anna's face and in her movements.

She turned to the man in black.

"If you'd care to come with me."

And followed by the man in black and with Anna trailing uncertainly behind she left the room and with almost regal self-possession she mounted the stairs without ever having to glance down to make sure of her footing. Her back was ramrod straight but inside things crumbled and fell or were painfully rent and somehow she knew they were all of great importance but just why and how and to what degree, she couldn't quite comprehend. She only realised she had suffered a total, bloody defeat at the hand of Mrs Platt. Mrs Platt, at best, a surly, unwilling servant, was always formidable. Aroused and as well armed as she now was, she could prove extremely dangerous.

She led them into David's room and stepped aside to allow the man in black an unobstructed view.

He stood in the doorway and his eyes flickered expertly over the scene. He showed no emotion nor was there any in his voice when he spoke. "Everything seems straightforward and simple enough Madam." And then hesitating for a fraction of a second he took a rolled-up metal tape measure from his jacket pocket.

"If you don't mind Madam. . . it's always best to be sure."

"No. I don't mind. Please carry on. . . . We're not in your way or anything?" Her voice was hesitant. There was nothing, she thought bitterly, imperious about it now. He expertly flicked out the tape to about two feet and swiftly measured the body on the bed, murmuring as he did so, "Two, four, five and a few inches." David she remembered had at one time measured over six foot. "Give a good clearance and all's well that ends well," he murmured unconsciously speaking aloud. "Yes. I'd say that's just about right, Madam." He flicked the tape and it slid like a snake back into its silver-bright case which the man in black returned to his jacket pocket. He whistled softly and, again, quite unconsciously. "It's always better to be sure than sorry. I could tell a story or two which would make your hair stand. . . ." He paused, realising where he was and who Gertrude was.

Gertrude clenched and unclenched her fists in inner desperation. "Why, in God's name, can't he get on with it," she howled silently.

The man glanced at her and assumed correctly that she hadn't in fact heard what he had just said. There was therefore, he felt, no need to apologise. He whistled softly again and rising on the tip of his feet swayed gently and almost imperceptibly. His eyes were fixed on David yet wildly focused rather than concentrating on any given detail. He furrowed his brow and frowned, the very picture of perplexity. Then, like a clouded sky clearing, his face relaxed, all tension draining away. He all but beamed. As it was triumph and gladness showed clearly in his eyes.

"The ring, Madam. The ring," he exclaimed, his ringing tones punning his word usage.

"What about it?" Gertrude asked turning to him in surprise.

"It looks valuable Madam. And very beautiful need I say, but are you sure you want it to go?"

Gertrude frowned. "Go?"

"Into the crematorium. . . . It will melt, you see, and be destroyed. . . it will, so to speak, render in the intense heat and the stone? The stone would be tarnished beyond recognition if not indeed reduced to powder."

The ring, she thought. My God, I must try and think clearly about it.

It was solid gold meant only to hold the lapis-lazuli stone which, itself streaked with gold, showed to such good effect against the precious metal. It was, she had been told, or more correctly Father who had made the purchase had been told, a very fine and rare piece of stone, the blue a shade lighter than was normally the case and the streaks of gold were as thin as thread and did not detract from the gold of the ring. It had been the family's gift to David on his birthday. He had volunteered and had been unhesitatingly accepted. It was the third year of war and the resolute conviction that it would be a short war had worn thin, yet they somehow hoped David would come through unscathed. No one specifically raised that point. It was just felt by everybody that a special gift should be bought to mark the occasion. A family council excluding David had been summoned and each had made their suggestion. "A pocket watch," she said. "A super pocket watch with a lid to protect the glass and dial. . . . Gold with an enamelled decoration on it. . . . A pastoral scene or something bright and cheerful like an eighteenth-century Court scene with ladies in elegant dress and men in embroidered waistcoats and brocade shortcoats and silken breeches and stockings and shoes of the finest leather." Father: "I rather thought a fine gold cigarette case or even a hip flask might be more suitable." Faintly offended when no one squealed with delight at his suggestion. David didn't even then smoke, still less drink. . . at least not to her knowledge. "A ring," Mother suggested passing through the drawing-room with a bunch of flowers for one of the numerous vases she had stationed strategically throughout the house with the result that one was being constantly surprised and delighted at flowers and greenery arranged in the most unexpected places. "A gold ring," she said. "Coiled in an ancient manner and with a beautiful stone." She stopped in her tracks as if horror struck, pain allied to mental pictures of carnage and horror. "Oh, *not* a bloodstone!. . . Something wonderful to complement his beauty. Lapis-lazuli to suit his eyes." And oblivious to their excited congratulations, her eyes hazed or almost glazed and safely distant once more from them and the small, multitudinous things which caused her such terrible anguish, she left them to their plotting and went her way.

"Let it go," Gertrude said with savage decision. "Let it go!"

The blue, she thought even as she listened to what she was saying and the vehemence with which she said it, the blue is too beautiful, too reminiscent of his eyes and their extraordinary luminosity whenever he was even faintly aroused sexually. Let it be rendered, she thought bitterly. Let the beautiful blue stone be reduced to powder or otherwise destroyed utterly. Let the gold go also!

The man in black stopped rocking on his feet and coughed a dry cough, a false cough. An acquired cough. Part of his stock in trade. His voice was unwarrantly harsh as he spoke.

"I'm afraid it can't be done, Madam. Not at all. . . . You see, it's against regulations. Firstly because the presence of foreign bodies in the clothing of the deceased, such as rings or watches or cigarette cases. . . that sort of thing, is strictly forbidden by the company. You'd be astonished Madam, at what some people want to send into the crematorium together with the remains," he gratuitously informed her. "Beyond belief some of the daft things they want to send along." She thought him rather too familiar but felt it wisest not to comment.

"I don't mind," she protested, "I really don't mind at all."

He shook his head rather gleefully, she thought. This man delights in his job. He delights in this macabre conversation. He has no idea whatever of the human pity involved. No inkling of what constitutes bereavement. He relishes the whole damn thing, quietly and very, very deeply.

"There's the legal aspect Madam. I mean, I accept that the ring on the gentleman's finger is legally his in every sense of the word and so do you. But what proof, what legal proof have we got that it legally belongs to him and he wished it to be so destroyed? Proof, Madam, legal proof I'm talking about. . . ." He paused with only the slightest glimmer of pleasure in his eyes. "Did the gentleman make a will? A will signed, sealed and delivered, so to speak?"

"No," she snapped shortly. "He did not! And," she continued in cold anger, "there is nothing to dispute. It is my wish that the ring remains where it is. I'll give you written permission which will stand up in any court of law if you insist!" Her voice shook with fury. "And surely that is that?"

He shook his head slowly from side to side as though he had spent endless hours practising the gesture to imbue it with undue solemnity.

"Sorry Madam, but past experience involving our company in legal action has compelled us to adopt our present attitude. Under no circumstances whatever can the ring remain where it is. It has to come off."

A silence descended and she heard distantly the rustle of tree and bush and, or so she imagined, sedges — all the tiny sounds which constitute the so called silence of the countryside.

Rigor mortis has set in. As it is the ring was simply placed on his finger and his fingers enfolded to hold it in position as his fingers were nothing but bones covered lightly with a minimum of flesh and a layer of skin. They will, she realised with rising nausea, have to break his finger or fingers to get it off and since his hand is at a right angle to his body at the elbow, they might well have to break his arm also.

She stared in horror at the man in black and saw him as something filthy and obscene, relishing as he did his task with such latent glee. You dirty little bastard, she thought, you filthy little swine all in beetle black. . . . You . . . you cockroach. . . . You knew all along this had to be done.

Aloud she said, "Take it off. And when my brother's body is coffined, kindly inform me."

He bowed, slightly. "Very good Madam."

He went to follow her from the room. She turned at

him and snapped, "Is there something else?"

"I need the, eh, the assistance of my colleagues at this stage Madam."

"I'll send them up," she replied shortly, thinking dear God no . . . don't let them have to break his fingers or his arm, and mentally she heard them being broken with the clean, dry snap of dry sticks being snapped across the knee or kindling snapping under the merest pressures of one's fingers.

She approached the drawing-room. There was no sign of Anna or Mrs Platt, she thought thankfully, and then entered the dining-room and found the man's colleagues. They were huddled over a much folded paper now unfolded and spread out on the dining table like so many brazen schoolboys huddled excitedly over a pornographic magazine. All were smoking with scant attention to the ashtrays carefully placed about the room. They started rather guiltily when they saw her and smoothed down their jackets and adjusted their black ties and hid their cigarettes in the palms of their hands. Again she was reminded of brazen schoolboys.

"Please go upstairs. The first landing. You are all wanted."

They nodded deferentially and began to sneak from the room. The third of their number trying unsuccessfully to ram the hastily folded newspaper into the back pocket of his trousers.

They fled, or rather scurried, away like chastened mice.

She opened a window to allow air to enter the smoke-filled room and gratefully sank into an armchair in the corner by the fireplace. A gentle breeze blew playfully, soothingly against the nape of her neck and part of her face. I wouldn't mind dying, she thought wearily. Not really. I wouldn't mind slipping into oblivion and have this terrible burden taken from my shoulders. . . . And she thought of Anna, coldly and dispassionately at first. She thought of her perfectly white body. Her skin, silken soft and smooth. Virtually without blemish of any kind. That night they had chatted when Anna first arrived with her tiny suitcase, her gas mask in its box and her shell, sea shell. . . . And they had managed to communicate even though Anna knew little English and her French was far from adequate. And instead of two, solemn-faced individuals seated across a dining table from each other, trying desperately to converse or establish contact of some kind in between very heavy silences and innumerable offers of cups of tea, lively, they chatted in fits and starts and each defined their role without inhibition or verbal expression. She the lover and, as yet, Anna the loved, because she had fallen instantly in love with Anna and desired her childish, unformed body. . . . And Anna, on her part, had only begun to *like* her. First they had eaten and then, thrilled, Anna asked to be taken on a tour of the house which was big and in many respects beautiful and the rather taken-for-granted furniture was for the most part antique, rare and valuable. All of which delighted Anna who kept saying excitedly how much, much more beautiful than anything the Müllers had in their house. Afterwards they explored the garden, now neglected and overgrown since the death of Mother and the departure of Mr Cowles who, now dead himself, had stayed on for a pittance when he could have retired in relative security and plentitude but was too devoted to Mother to do so. The quiet, gnarled, wizened old man knew how desperately Mother needed the garden in her sad, mad way, and so he had stayed to the bitter end.

But she had forgotten the enchantment an overgrown garden holds for the young. An enchantment bordering on the magical if not mystical. It appealed in some odd way to depths within themselves they never knew existed. It awoke their dormant imagination, their sleeping innocence, and left it unbridled and free to romp and to construct that most important of childish things, a world confined and constricted by the limits of their imagination. It was not without an element of the hideous and the downright brutal.

She and David had played in the abandoned gardens of a derelict mansion nearby where a pond, almost choked with water-lillies, exercised a fascination for them they found impossible to resist, despite father's innumerable warnings and who knew perfectly well of their 'secret' garden, having possibly played there years before when he himself was a boy. David had once sought to get one of the water-lillies not yet fully opened but just about to do so.

"It will look superb, Bunch," he had said, "in your bedroom in a simple, large glass dish. It will be simply marvellous to watch it open gradually in response to sunlight." He had nearly drowned in his efforts and she had saved him by simply lying prone on the edge of the pond and throwing her cardigan to David while she held on for grim life to one sleeve, allowing him to grasp the other.... (What was she doing with a cardigan on what she remembered as a splendidly sunny summer's afternoon?) David, for once thoroughly frightened, grasped the sleeve thrown to him and she, by summoning extraordinary strength, had managed to pull him from the pond. It had silted with a black foul-smelling matter which threatened to drag him down and eventually close over him like quicksand, smothering him to death. And the horrible possibility which she could all too vividly imagine had spurred her on, despite the fact that that on which she lay was slowly crumbling away beneath her and there was a real danger it would collapse altogether and pitch her also into the deceptively beautiful pond with its vast spreads of exquisite water-lillies. She managed to rescue him and, beaming, he ruffled her hair and hugged her and possibly for the first time called her 'old thing' saying, "Thanks, old thing. You're a sport. A real sport." And his tanned legs and the greater part of his shorts caked with foul-smelling slime, they went to the brook which was pristine and shot with silver and ran over a shallow stretch, sweetly musical in a way which so appealed to the young minds, as in time, she realised, it did to the aged. And David had stripped and she had turned aside while naked he washed his shorts and shirt in the shallows because he was shy and had no wish to have her see him naked. And she had laid them out on the grass and they had dried with remarkable rapidity while David tried to hide his nakedness like the disgraced Adam, just expelled from paradise in the Italian paintings, tried to hide his nakedness with his hands shielding his genitals. Then when dressed and his natural exuberance and self-confidence fully restored... no, not fully restored . . . for one or two nights afterwards she heard him call her name in terror and as he relived the moments of horror and what could have resulted in a horrible death for him. "Bunch, Bunch!" he cried. "I'm going under!" And she adored him because from that sleeping, secret part of him, the one window to the soul, he had called to her in his extreme distress. With the lace curtains barely billowing in the soft, night air, she stole into his room and gently woke him but only after she touched his bare upper-body which was awash with sweat like ever-separating and isolating drops of mercury in the pale white light of night. . . and gently stoked his nipples, and fear, only fear of waking him prevented her from touching him where she most wanted to touch him. . . at the genitals and the groin already showing wheaten hair fairer than that on his head. The scrotum hanging sideways and like a lax, summer flower about to flower fully, the limp penis with its exquisitely pink and purple tip, lying there like some handsome gift between his thighs which were smooth and tanned and masculine, giving the impression of great thrust. She pulled back the sweat-drenched sheet and quietly examined coolly and closely the details of his nakedness even as he thrashed and choked and called desperately, "Bunch, Bunch. . . I'm going under!" Then she gently woke him. He stared at her as if she were a being of apparitional beauty, and smiled, and pulling the damp sheets closer about him outlining in marvellous detail his splendidly proportioned body saying, "Thanks old thing . . . . Thanks a million Bunch," and indicated that she should lie by him on the bed. She did so. He kissed her on the forehead and acutely aware of the warmth of his body apparent through the dampened sheet, she fell asleep in his arms. . . and quite without knowing it, she had fallen in love with him. Her brother David.

Then when his shirt had dried and his shorts, they went and found a place where the brook trickled through, rather than ran over, stones and pebbles. Minnows, silver-streaked and with white under-bellies, flecked vivid crimson markings, thrashed with primeval force and urgency to gain the upper reaches where the water was deeper and afforded greater safety in which to mature. Foraging about in the old conservatory of the derelict house, David found a jamjar and they caught a great many of the minnows and, carrying them off in triumph, they entered the walled garden and laid the jamjar on a pebbled walk and watched them turn and twist and flip and flap, terror causing their already bulging, lidless eyes to bulge further. Then with the calamitous brutality of the innocent, word unspoken, they slipped their hands into the jar and taking a smooth, silver minnow dashed it against the massive walls of the garden, killing it instantly. As though drunk on some sort of lust, they killed them all, one by one, with wanton savagery and then as though confronting the stranger in themselves and one another, they stared long and hard at each other. In silence and in shame.

But Anna had experienced only joy at the freedom afforded her by the overgrown garden, difficult for an adult to penetrate with ease because little trimmed shrubs had grown sizeably and trees had matured with remarkable speed and virility. She had found their little pond which never boasted water-lillies and was in no way remarkable. She found also in the farthest corner of the garden the wretched grotto Cowles had built for Mother under her strict supervision and which had a niche for a statue of the Virgin of Lourdes. White-robed with a white veil draped about her head and shoulders, a blue band about her waist, a golden rose at her right foot. Hands, slender and delicate and supplicatingly clasped in prayer, eyes turned heavenwards in an attitude of intercession. Mother's last wretched refuge in the last years of her life, a lapse into a private religion which sometimes grotesquely parodied the religion of her fathers' because she had been a member of an old aristocratic family, recorded long before the Doomsday Book was written. Their name figured prominently in the history of the many wars at home and abroad and boringly and predictably in her history books.

Here, when the evening star was bright on a fine summer's evening, with lighted candle she entered into the sad, obsessive ritual of one in extreme dementia.

A member of an aristocratic English Catholic family — how she had loathed the Irish, whom she termed pig-sty Catholics — distant and now peripheral to the core of the family which had served with both dignity and satisfaction their royal masters, be they Protestant or Catholic. Through all the turbulent years of religious strife which astonishingly adhered to the throne of England, they managed by some agility of mind or mental gymnastics to please the sovereign greatly, with the result they retained their titles and their many thousands of acres of rich pastureland once belonging to the Church to which they owed spiritual allegiance.

She had married outside the Church and her happiness had seemed ample compensation for the excommunication she had automatically incurred. She bore two healthy children and lost one, a tiny weakling fated never to know long life and which died young, and the death of the boy marked Mother's slow descent into madness. She had worshipped him and nursed him with the desperation of the mentally unhinged and when he died she held him tightly for hours on end, refusing to abandon in death what she had refused to abandon in life, until he was taken forcibly from her and quietly buried in the local churchyard. She took to haunting the nearest Catholic church which was in a town some twenty miles distance, built in a seedy, working-class area, and whose parishioners were largely Irish immigrants. She attended Mass, confessed and was refused absolution. She again attended Mass and with the other devout communicants she knelt at the altar rails, head bowed in devout prayer ready to receive at any moment the thin, consecrated host she now hungered for unimaginably. But the celebrant, a thickset Irishman with great tufts of black hair sprouting from both of his ugly, over-developed ears and coating the back of his hands and each of his fingers, refused her communion though she remained at the rail long after he had ceased to distribute and he had had to pass her at least four times to cope with the large number receiving. She remained a still, solitary figure at the rail all through the second part of Mass and remained there in pain and in prayer even when the Mass had ended and the congregation had begun to disperse. He met her at the door as she left. The big, rather apish man said gruffly but not unkindly, "You may attend Mass as much as you wish Mrs Gaunt, but you will never again receive communion from the hands of God's annointed, until you publicly repent of your sin and make your peace with God and Holy Mother, The Church."

"I hadn't intended returning," Mother had told him,

slipping on her tight kid gloves. "And I never shall," she said, "whatever the circumstances," and stricken she had walked away. Her family disowned her and where possible penalised her even to the extent of requesting her to refrain from attending family christenings and burials. She learnt in time of the death of her father and mother and then, through the war years, of the death of all her five brothers in the columns of *The Times*. So, deprived of all the sources of consolation which the average person could normally hope to call upon with certainty, she sought to battle alone and was forced into the absurd excesses of the strange, pathetic rituals she performed before the statue of the Virgin in the garden, while Cowles, ever faithful, kept watch.

Mother dying —
a still, limp form on the bed, her head barely denting the pillows, her eyes wide and luminous as if lit by an inner radiance one would like to term spiritual but was in fact the response of her body to the coming extinguishment of the light of life. By her, on a bedside locker, a vase of common wild flowers a nurse had kindly picked for her and which, seen out of their natural context, were striking and individual. The water was fresh and crystal clear and, Gertrude remembered vividly, distorted the image of the lower stems in accordance with some law or other of optics. Mother dying but silent. Very silent. A sad silence which enveloped her and them and which they dreaded she would die without breaking.

They called her.

David and she, "Mother, Mother," gently, whisperingly but in utter desperation, dreading that the frail spirit which barely seemed to linger on might depart and she would be silent for ever and always. Realising with considerable pain how much they loved and cherished her. Above all, realising how much they needed her, the vague, insubstantial figure which was amongst them but never seemed *of* them. Calling, whispering, imploring, begging, beseeching and at the same time watching the chest which seemed to expand and constrict less and less with each breath she took. "Mother,

Mother, Mother . . . ."

Father enquiring *sotto voce*, of a nurse, if there was a
Catholic priest available, preferably English. And being
assured by the nurse in a soft, unmistakably Irish accent
of obvious dedication and compassion that "yes" there
was and should she summon him? Father nodded and the
nurse hurried away and then they heard urgent, light foot-
steps and a tall, grey-haired man, bowed and old, with an
oval, not unlovely face, a sharp nose and lively grey-blue
eyes, quintessentially English, entered the room, his manners
immediately recognisable not simply being present, but
present in distinction. He nodded gently in recognition,
blessed himself, hurriedly unfurled a slim, purple stole and
having kissed the cross embroidered on it mid-centre, he draped
it about his neck, its gold-fringed edging hanging freely in
front, less so behind. He gently touched the woman on the
bed who opened her eyes and smiled at him and then closed
them again. He turned to Father and they had a hurried con-
sultation and then as Father nodded agreement, he signalled
them to withdraw. He set up a portable altar on the bedside
locker. It consisted of a cross-shaped box which opened up to
show on the inside of the lid the figure of Christ crucified and
on the lower half, two small candles, somberly and deeply
amber, and some cotton wool and two round, silver boxes.
They and, much to his chagrin, Father, were asked to leave and
having left they heard distinctly the low intonations of
prayers in Latin, the beginnings of a last confession. It con-
tinued so for what seemed a very long time and then the
door opened and beckoning to them urgently the priest
whispered, "Please come . . . I fear she is fading." They
entered and Mother was fully conscious and to their joy
recognised them and naming each by name she took her
leave of them. . . her eyes so intensely bright, so irradiantly
lovely and all-forgiving. Her last words. To Father. "You
have been very kind to me all my life. I forgive you." She
smiled a sad, secretive smile. "I forgive you everything,"
then she died and the priest imparted a final blessing.
Solemn and sonorous the Latin phraseology falling into the
abyss of silence which now surrounded Mother and forever
would. They fell gently, beautifully and though one knew

them to be spurious, they seemed as rain to parched earth, balm to an open wound.

And Father.

Father bowed his head and wept brokenly, for he was as they all knew, Mother most of all — a kind and generous man, a diligent father and in all his business transactions as honourable as could be expected. He was very, very much in love with Mother . . . . But Father, they knew — Father had never been faithful.

They left the room.

David and she,

she twisting a handkerchief between her hands and aware of how ugly she looked when she wept or snivelled. She tried not to cry and instead made a series of grunt-like noises which alone signalled her grief, and David, weeping freely, kicked at the wall of the corridor which was painted in two distinct shades of slime green, muttering, "Oh, fuck, oh fuck, oh fuck it all Bunch . . . Why here and like that?"

They allowed her Christian burial in consecrated ground. Granting in death a dignity they had so vindictively denied her in life. Her grave was under spreading trees well matured and handsome in full foliage. It would, they appreciated, be beautiful in the spring and glorious in the summer. They left her there in that lovely summer place. They swore they would never visit her grave.

Nor did they.

Anna gazed with profound pity at the crumbling face of the plaster Virgin, the greater part of the right-hand side fallen away, exposing the central metal framework on which the body had hung. The other half of the face retained an eye, enlarged and grotesque looking as if it were meant to portray someone hideously afflicted or a figure of Greek mythology with its eyes gorged out and havoc wrought on other parts of the body by vengeful gods or blind, unrelenting fate. Ivy had wound its way around the body of the figure giving it a greater sense of the forlorn, the abandoned, the decayed.

Anna gazed and remembered the crisp, burnt bodies she

had seen that morning so long ago she couldn't really quite remember when.... But vividly remembering how those victims had looked. How much more like plucked and roasted fowl rather than humans, they had struck her.

She immediately loved the pock-marked face of the crumbling figure and its entwining ivy and the rank weeds high all about it, and always endearing to her, the vivid red and orange poppies which spelt death and carnage to her young mind.

"Who is it?" she asked.

Gertrude bit her lip and thought she had better not get too deeply involved in what was, after all, quite a complex matter.

"It's the Virgin of Lourdes. The Virgin who allegedly appeared to a young peasant girl sometime in the last century."

Anna thought, her brow furrowed. "She looks sad. Was she?"

Completely taken unaware, Gertrude replied with a certitude she hadn't thought she possessed. "Yes, I rather think she was. Sad. Very sad indeed." And then feeling psychic wounds had been sufficiently reopened, all unwittingly by the arrival of Anna, she said, "Now come along. It's late. You must have a bath and then go to bed. We can start discussing all sorts of things tomorrow."

Anna nodded with the disturbing solemnity which was fast showing itself as one of her stronger characteristics.

"May I come here please," she asked and as Gertrude was about to reply rather expansively, "Why yes, of course," she added, "alone," and the force of that one word struck Gertrude with the impact of a well-aimed bullet. It was not, she realised as she literally staggered in shock, it was not intended to wound or even bruise, but it unmistakably showed there were certain reserves or perhaps preserves of the mind and imagination which her new pupil guarded jealously and possibly with every reason, would brook no trespass.

She gazed at the solemn brown eyes watching her steadily. "Yes," she said evenly, "You may come here as often as you like. Alone. Consider it your private demesne. I promise I shall never come here whether you are absent or not unless you specifically invite me."

Anna nodded agreement and simply said, "Thank you," and impulsively she stretched her hand to be taken by Gertrude and taking it Gertrude was, she realised, nakedly and unashamedly grateful for the human contact it afforded her. For the warmth, the love it might possibly imply, and she felt an upsurgence of hope she had long thought of abandoned or indeed dead. True, she daily attended to David and all his bodily needs but David's body was cold to touch. Only the heart was warm. Even, she reflected miserably . . . even his loins were cold. Ice-cold and lifeless. She knew. She had felt them more than once and in times of intense isolation and desolation following Father's death, she had gently tried to arouse that spent member, the very vigour of which had meant so much to her in her earlier years and aroused desires which time had enforced and made stronger rather than reduced. Nothing whatever could stir it to life. He lingered on, in, she thought, remembering her mother's belief, in limbo, a state of joy without bliss.

There had been that difficult moment after tea when she had taken Anna upstairs and Anna had noticed the subdued light of the lamp which was always kept burning in David's room day and night. It showed as a thin strip of yellow or amber light, such as might be visible under a nursery door.

"What's that?" Anna enquired directly, almost lightly. "Is there someone in there?"

"Yes," Gertrude replied, realising instinctively that only the most searing honesty and outright candour would gain Anna's respect and gaining Anna's respect was the means of obtaining her trust and affection. And in time, possibly her love. "My brother David is in there. He's asleep. He sleeps all the time. . . day and night. You see, he was injured many years ago in the Great War and since then he has hardly woken. . . that is, *really* woken. He sustained spinal damage and that is why he is the way he is. . . . I have to care for him day and night. . . and I shall have to care for him until the day he dies."

Anna hugged her impulsively. "I'll help you take care of him. I promise. I promise. May I see him before I have my bath?"

She nodded consent and led Anna along the landing with its threadbare carpet, praying quietly that David's bowels hadn't moved since last she looked in on him, or a bedsore discharged some foul matter which would possibly cause Anna to be repelled or sickened by the sight and smell of David. And it was important, desperately important, to her and her capacity for love of Anna, that Anna at the very least should like David, if only a little.

She opened the door and they entered the room bathed in its subdued light and through the windows which were partially opened, a fresh breeze wafted through the room and David smelt not repellently but slightly sweet in a mild and pleasant way. To her, Gertrude, the scent was that of faintly scented roses, though it wasn't even rose time and there were no other flowers in the room. There never had been, she realised to her amazement. Anna broke from her and stood at the end of the bed, and hands straight down on either side, palms turned in and pressed against her thighs, she subjected the ravished figure on the bed to the closest scrutiny and Gertrude found herself almost irresistibly drawn to pray, that please God, make at least her not be repelled by the sight of him. And then, voice a little too blithe, and highly pitched, asking, "Well, what do you think of him?"

And turning to her Anna said simply, "I think he's very beautiful. . . very, very beautiful." Adding, "I like him. I love him."

Gertrude cried and fell to her knees and kissed and kissed her in a welter of emotions — relief, joy and gratitude. All flooded her joyously and she sought to give them expression.

"No," she said, "he's not beautiful now. . . but once he was. Very beautiful indeed. Once, when he and I were young." She wept freely and embraced Anna: "He was beautiful then. . . in every way. Later, I shall show you photographs and some sketches and paintings of him. And I shall tell you stories about him and what he did and said. And how very, very much I loved him. David my brother."

Anna allowed the emotional torrent of words to cease, the hysterical kissing of her fingers by Gertrude, before touching Gertrude on the forehead, on her lips and then on her covered breasts.

"What," she asked, "is his name?"

"David," she replied, adding idiotically, "David, the mighty king."

Anna nodded her head in approval and whispered the phrase, "David. The mighty king."

Watching her so avidly, so hungrily as she took off her clothes and stood naked by the bath, aware of Gertrude's scrutiny and not at all afraid of what was now rank worship of her firm, young, girlish body. Gertrude washing her. Gently lapping the water over her blemishless skin. Watching it trickle down her back, dividing into two streams to pass down beyond the spinal column and on down to the cleft above the anus. Washing her developing breasts which were so humanly and wonderfully soft and evoked in her the hunger once so easily aroused and appeased by David. Feeling between her thighs. The ever-increasing urgency to have her moisturing vagina probed and penetrated. Feeling. Feeling intensely the intense hunger far up in her lower body, in that part of her body meant to know seeding by man. Biting her lip and experiencing a deep, inner shame. A sense of betrayal. Of herself and of David. But only fleetingly ... only very fleetingly and past pleasure gave way to the pleasurable immediate moment. Touching Anna playfully with her soaped palms; moving her hands about her breasts, her flat, surprisingly muscular stomach and her thighs already being cushioned by warm, attractive flesh. Biting her lips in guilt and breathing deeply and praying, "Oh God, no!" The responsibility ... The possible consequences! And then, in her extreme hunger and desire, gently caressing the mound between her thighs and gently, very gently, introducing her finger and probing ... gently, gently, arousing in herself and as could be clearly seen in her eyes — in Anna, exquisite pleasure. Anna smiling faintly about the lips and with a calculation that was stunning and straightforward, seizing her finger and lustily driving it into her body and holding it there and then, body dripping wet, clambering over the side of the bath and clinging to Gertrude's left thigh, manipulated her body to obtain maximum effect and satisfaction. Pressing

her small, thin lips bluntly against her and kissing with a
passion which was both frightening and astounding in one
so young and yet which was so pleasing, and yes, satisfied
a hunger of the soul she had never admitted to but had tried
to obliterate from her consciousness as though it arose from
part of her which was not human and could not therefore be
a part of her physical or mental make-up, her being. She
thought of it as an inner aridity fated to be forever arid. But
now stone blossomed, aridity greened. There in the bathroom
as she opened her mouth and felt Anna's tongue looped
about hers and then slipped and slithered sensuously under
and over it, exploring avidly the cavity of the mouth as
deeply as possible.

Succumbing totally there on the bathroom floor with
nothing but towelling wrenched out of the linen cupboard
and thrown hastily on the cold linoleum and, hastily baring
her upper-body, proffering the breasts in turn to be suckled
upon or bitten teasingly, pleasingly, sexually. And then un-
covering her whole body as she had only ever done previous-
ly to David so many, many times. To David and only David
at his superb best, his muscular body rippling as he lithely
approached and erect between his thighs the rampant phallus
which was to haunt her dreams and she had visions, irrational
visions, of David arisen, renewed, made whole again. Prepar-
ing for the mount while in gratitude and delight she prepared
her body and parted her thighs to receive him. Humbly. But
with great joy.

Discovering to her surprise in the desolation which follow-
ed David's illness, his slide down into the nether world in
which he was to exist for the remainder of his life that she,
like him, was attracted to people of her own sex ... in
dreams. Only in dreams did she find in the love of her kind
some surcease, some easing of the pain which had left her as
though detruncated or her body so mutilated and paining as
though a large segment of it — her right shoulder and arm —
had been reefed away by some savage animal and she bled pro-
fusely and wondered why those about her could not see,
never notice her wound or imagine her pain.

Lying there in the bathroom, and having Anna reciprocate
her passion. Biting gently on her breasts which despite her

years were still firm and upright and down to the gentle folds
of her stomach and beyond her thighs and having her feast
there with an urgency she found at once both appallingly
direct and demanding. Realising that for all her appearance of
hurt innocence, and Anna she *knew* was intrinsically both
hurt and innocent, she had nevertheless long before been
initiated sexually in varying forms. She responded readily to
stimulus and knew how to arouse and to satisfy the deepest
sexuality in another. She, Gertrude, experiencing under the
expert probing of Anna's touch and her warm mouth about
her vagina, orgasms which she had not experienced for years
and which she allowed only to surface in her dream-state.

Bathing her again and joining her in the bath, each washing
each other with a happy sensuality which was like rain to
drought-afflicted land. Experiencing in many ways tiny
expansions of the mind like a near-withered plant putting
forth new and tender growth. Vowing that night when they
were naked in her bed that she would never again suffer such
deprivations as she had known since David's illness, and
vowing furthermore that she would never yield Anna to any
living soul. Anna stirring to half-consciousness in the pre-
dawn darkness when the room was at its coldest and the
breeze from the open window caused them to curl in upon
each other and Anna had commenced her fondling of her
pubic hair and had commenced her arousal and she had fully
responded and experienced again a sense of the deeply mira-
culous, a sense of living, of being made whole and one again.
Gratitude swelled in her for such sexual delights and for the
simple fact that now her long days of nothing but the servi-
tude of attendance to David's needs had purpose, a beginning
and an end, and astonishingly the years ahead which she
considered as holding nothing for her other than a slow
descent into decay and eventual death, now had meaning and
the reasonable anticipation of joys to come. Her deeply felt
need to love and be loved could be, were in fact, being fulfill-
ed. The situation, she realised, was not without danger but
danger was something she could and would do battle with.
Exposure and disgrace she would hazard. The prize was life
itself. Life as against mere existence.

Summoning Mrs Platt, her face frigid and mask-like,

wringing her hands unconsciously, instructing her clearly that
she was not to 'do' the two bedrooms on the second floor
(she was already forbidden entry to David's room under any
circumstances), and Mrs Platt's eyes narrowed and glinted
momentarily with the steel glint of battle. She carried a
sword, Gertrude realised, double-edged and honed to perfec-
tion and close to hand for use whenever she, Mrs Platt,
should choose to use it. Her deadpan voice; her slight curtsey,
"Yes Madam . . . will that be all Madam?" and on being told
"yes," that was all, and "yes," she might go. And go she did
and Gertrude never for one moment failed to realise that she
would draw her conclusions from what had been said and
that those conclusions would most likely be correct. She had,
she knew, delivered herself bound hand and foot into the
hands of a woman who felt betrayed by life and who as a
result had an almost infinite capacity for the vindictive and
splenetic. Given the opportunity she wouldn't hesitate to
vent her feelings on those she believed had wronged her.

I have offended her pride, she told herself. And with poor
people that is the one unpardonable sin, the transgression
that cannot be absolved, no matter what retribution is offer-
ed or penance undertaken.

A soft rap on the door brought her quickly back to the
present and its problems. "Please come in," she said quietly.
The door opened and the man in black stood there. She
nodded, knowing there was no explanation needed. She rose
conscious of that dream-like quality, that sense of unreality
which underlines the events of greatest importance in the
human life cycle, including the transition from life to death.
It can't possibly be happening, a part of her mind whispered
in fright. It can and it is, answered another interior voice, the
voice of reality itself. And what cannot be denied has to be
accepted, however unpleasant or unjust that reality may be.

The man in black stood aside to let her pass. She was
about to go upstairs when Anna entered the hall. The sunlight
struck her as she passed over the threshold from the lighted
area of the porch which harboured a mixture of red and
green and pale yellow filtered through the tinted panes of

glass. She looked unearthly beautiful and, yes, like Mother's crumbling statue of the Virgin, full of the pity of the world and compassion beyond measure. She carried in her hands a bunch of wild flowers and some which were rank weeds which had a charm and a beauty of their own.

"For David," she said simply and Gertrude nodded and taking Anna by the arm began the slow ascent of the stairs, the upward path to her personal Golgotha thinking how apt, how bitterly apt, was the Christian metaphor which presented itself. She remembered with vehemence her Gethsemane which had lasted for over twenty years and realised that for her afflictions she could never hope to know an Easter joy. They were on about the sixth step when they heard the door to the kitchen open noisily and Mrs Platt approached haughtily, her 'good' high-heeled shoes tapping her defiant progress. She was unaccountably dressed all in black with the exception of flesh-coloured stockings and a headscarf which showed a brightly coloured hunting scene. Gertrude reacted as though stung, deeply shocked, as if Mrs Platt had appeared dressed as a circus clown and begun some outrageous antics calculated to arouse the merriment and laughter of excited, anticipating children. You foul bitch, she thought silently. You foul, demeaning bitch. You are not above fouling your own nest, and then in a voice cold and even while feeling Anna's hand squeeze tightly about hers counteracting the fear, the very real fear she now felt before Mrs Platt, who unthinkingly had adopted a stance of a woman of the lower order about to brawl publicly and to the amusement of the other, she asked, "Was there something, Mrs Platt?"

Mrs Platt smiled. Actually beamed and then her face blackened and her mouth twisted in an ugly way. Her voice was even though cold and not without much-relished triumph. She spoke decisively, enunciating her words carefully, the carefully cultivated subservience of her years in her years of service totally absent.

"There is, Madam, lots of things I have to talk to you about but seeing the day it is, I'll hold my tongue for the time being."

"That's very considerate of you, Mrs Platt."

"I'll be leaving this house tonight for good and so will my

husband . . . and there are . . . ," she hesitated and looked so brazenly at Anna, the man in black in turn felt impelled to look at her. "But before I do leave, for good like, there are things I want straightened out." She again hesitated and drew a deep breath. "There's the question of assault . . . and battery . . . You struck me, Madam, without provocation or justification of any kind . . . that's assault, Madam."

"Mrs Platt, please . . . " Gertrude's plea, wrung from her, ended on a high note of hysteria and fear. Mrs Platt stared at her and then her eyes blinked rapidly like those of a tabby cat. Her lower jaw dropped and her exposed mouth looked plainly obscene.

"Not now, you wretched woman. You utter, stupid fool. You liced beggar on horseback. Not now! Later, woman . . . later! At a more suitable time!"

Gertrude was screaming and it echoed on and on as it rose towards the quietude which seemed clustered under the high ceiling above and which in time would absorb them as they eventually did all sound.

Mrs Platt blinked even more rapidly, blanched and stuttered, "I'll be back, Madam. I'll be back with my brother . . . and you'll regret this to your dying day."

"Summon your dead from their graves, woman, and bring them along," Gertrude was screaming in fury again. "Bring who you damn well like, only get out of this house instantly you insensitive oaf, or I'll pitch you out myself!" Gertrude made a slight move as if to descend. Anna tightened her clasp restrainingly.

Mrs Platt backed away . . . slowly, but decidedly, pulling on a pair of black kid gloves as she did so. "I'll be back," she swore blackly, "And I swear on my bible oath you won't like it one bit, nor will that tramp beside you." She nearly toppled backwards into the porch, regained her standing and turning sharply to the right, left the house. They heard her footsteps on the gravel. They were plainly not the footsteps of a peaceable or well-intentioned person.

Gertrude took a deep breath and Anna, still clutching her hand, ascended the stairs, passed along the short landing and entered David's room and stared in disbelief at the figure in the coffin.

On her instructions David's body had been dressed in his uniform with the little coloured ribbon which denoted that the wearer was the recipient of the V.C. The uniform fitted particularly well considering that David's body had shrunk so much over the years. Not shrunk so much as wasted. Then she realised in dull despair it had been made to fit. What she found so astonishing and revolting was the fact that his face had been made up in a vain effort to duplicate the healthy appearance of a living person. The result was grotesque and hideous. And sickening. Very sickening. One hand lay crossed upon the other on his chest. There was no sign of the ring on any finger.

Gertrude drew a few breaths and fought the rising sense of anger and outrage causing her upper body to constrict and bring painful pressure to her heart. "What," she demanded, pointing to the figure in the coffin, "What, or rather who, is that wretched dummy in that uniform?"

Her question was met with stunned silence by most and by what appeared to be pain and perplexity by the man in black. He blinked rapidly rather as Mrs Platt had done. His companions moved swiftly and silently to his side and, like the Fates, they conferred.

"Who," Gertrude repeated, "is that wretched figure in the coffin with rouge and make-up and lipstick?" She laughed hysterically. "Lipstick!" she exclaimed, "Oh no! It simply can't be true!"

She put her hands to her head and sat on a nearby chair and rocked to and fro, oscillating between hysterical laughter and strangulated grief.

The man in black affected astonishment. His two companions hovered in the background more like figures of Fate than ever. He spoke rather stiffly and offendedly. "We do find, Madam, that most people like their loved one to look as natural . . ."

"Do not call him that," Gertrude screamed with the full force of her lungs."

"As possible. Life-like if you like Madam. Much as they remember them being in life." He spoke like a clockwork piece at a sideshow with a gramophone disc concealed in the bowels of his body. "Our efforts are usually appreciated," he concluded rather limply.

Gertrude opened her mouth to speak and found herself convulsed by hiccups. As though a magician who had once tucked it under the tail of his morning coat as part of his stock-in-trade, one of the men produced a glass of clear, fresh water which he thrust into Gertrude's hand and in a no-nonsense sort of voice ordered her to drink it, which Gertrude did and gasped in surprise when he thumped her broadly on the back with his open hand. The man in black wilted as though he thought his colleague had taken leave of his senses. The one remaining in the background moved his lips as if in prayer. Gertrude gasped and caught her breath. She found her hiccups gone. "Thank you," she said in frank admiration at the man's skill. "I am very much obliged to you." To all three she said, "Excuse me," and beckoning to Anna, whispered to her. Anna left the room.

Gertrude spoke quietly, authoritatively, and not without kindness.

"Gentlemen, I know you have a very difficult task and I do want to assure you I appreciate that you have tried to carry out that task as best you can, but I'm afraid I can't let my brother go ... ," she gestured to the rouge-faced figure in the coffin, "looking like that. My friend and I will see to things. In the meanwhile you all withdraw. We will summon you as soon as possible. I promise not to delay you unduly. There is a room next door where you can all sit down and if you wish, smoke to your heart's content." Her voice had unconsciously taken on what she dimly recognised as a regal tone and sitting on the edge of her chair and toying with a handkerchief with which she had tried to stifle her hysterical laughter, felt she must have looked and sounded very stupid indeed. Somewhat like the diminutive Queen Victoria who always gave her the impression *she* was seated with a ramrod up her rear passage. Obviously the men before her did not share that view of herself. They nodded with great solemnity as though indeed royally commanded and edging backwards from her, all but bowed before leaving the room. At the door the man in black plucked up sufficient courage and scurrying back whispered urgently,

"The medals, Madam. They're only there for..." He

hesitated. Plainly he had intended saying 'show' but thought better of it. "They're there as a mark of respect to the deceased. They won't be destroyed, I assure you ... I'll personally remove them before the coffin is finally closed."

She hadn't noticed the medals but they were there. Oddly she had noted only the V.C. ribbon and the absence of the ring. She shook her head gravely and said, "Thank you. I appreciate your kindness and consideration."

The man in black smiled weakly, swallowed hard and then muttered rapidly under his breath, "White spirits Madam, if you want to take off the make-up." He turned and scurried away to join his companions.

Anna had returned with a basin of steaming water and a towel. She had heard the exchange. "I'll get some white spirits. There's some in the garage. And I'll bring some strips of linen. They'll be more effective."

Touching Gertrude on the cheek with the fingers of one hand she again left the room. Silence descended in the room and seemed to centre on the coffined figure. "Poor David. I hoped it would all be solemn and measured and somewhat stately ... dignified if nothing else ... and here we are. Everything has descended to the level of farce, simple, outrageous farce." Unaware that she was talking aloud she continued, "Anna will soon be back . . . and we'll restore your rightful dignity." And she found herself crying silently because there was no god or prophet she believed in sufficiently to call upon to raise David from the dead and restore him to life and health.

Anna entered the room, the sleeves of her black dress rolled up. "I'll do it," she whispered, "You sit down and take things easy."

Gertrude sat down again and it suddenly occured to her that not only David's cremation but her harsh encounter with Mrs Platt were factors which marked the day as one of the greatest importance in her life, likely to alter her life as she had known it until now, possibly beyond recognition. With it came a swift fleeting intimation that she might not survive the day. She glanced lovingly at Anna and nodded her head in sad acceptance. There was Anna to be considered now. Soon David would cease to have any further claim on her time. Anna would displace him as the centre of life and the ends towards which she would struggle to survive.

Mrs Platt loomed large in her mind. The woman did in law have grounds for grievance. She would have to be bought off. Anna was legally still a minor and while that particular point might not be an issue in itself, there was, as far as she could remember, no legislation whatever governing the intimate relations between women. Mrs Platt would play heavily on the threat to drag the issue out into the public which might be ruinous to Anna and, at the least, distasteful to her. Crocker, she told herself, would take care of the whole thing. The old family solicitor had taken care of more than a few bits of dirty business for the family in his time, amongst them the illicit procurement of drugs in the early stages of David's illness and the sometimes sordid outcome of Father's affairs which all unhappily terminated in a squabble for money or valuable possessions of one kind or another. Crocker, she again reassured herself, would see to Mrs Platt. A lump sum of a few hundred and perhaps, perhaps a small weekly payment . . . a pension for services rendered over the years during which she discharged her duties with a fidelity and loyalty which was admirable and merited just reward.

"Good God!" she exclaimed and sat bolt upright. Anna, who was carefully drying David's face having removed most of the make-up, started in terror as though he, not she, had spoken.

"What is it?" she asked in terror.

"Oh, nothing really," Gertrude said, oblivious of the fright the girl had received. "It's just that I forgot all about Mr Chuckleworth. He's downstairs in Father's study. I'd better go and release him. Can you manage things here?" Anna nodded her head. "Good," said Gertrude. "I'll go and see to the old buff and send him on his way. I'll be back directly and then come hell or high water I'll see that David has a decent funeral and not a jack-in-the-box effort like a side show at some fifth-rate circus."

She hurried downstairs unaccountably afraid that Mr Chuckleworth might be snooping . . . yes, snooping. Prying about. Poking his nose into what didn't concern him. Not that Mr Chuckleworth was in any way like that. Oh no, indeed. But then she shared the family belief that all clerics were to some extent odd . . . and some of their oddities were less so than others.

She opened the door to the study. Mr Chuckleworth was nowhere to be seen though there on the table was his beautiful gold watch with its enamelled lid. It ticked distinctively in the quietness of the study undisturbed by the ticking of any other clock. In accordance with family custom every clock in the house had been stopped at the precise time of David's death. And would remain so until he was cremated.

"What will I do with the damn thing?" she thought irritably, rushing to the window to see if Mr Chuckleworth was anywhere in sight. There was no one to be seen. Nothing disturbed the stillness of the herbaceous border and those of its plants in flower. The pebbles lay perfectly undisturbed on the drive . . . smooth, and as she knew from her bare-footed summers of long ago, warm to the touch of bare flesh. "Oh well," she assured herself, "He'll be back for it." She slipped it into the drawer of the desk and carefully locking the drawer slipped the key behind the clock on the mantlepiece. If only I could make it appear like theft, she thought, and somehow implicate Mrs Platt. It would give me a hold over her . . . a rod to beat her back. Had she such a rod now she would beat the wretched woman black. The thought was foolish. She dismissed it instantly.

Anna called urgently. From the distance between them her voice sounded even more urgent, though thin and enfeebled. She returned to the room upstairs, half-expecting another disaster, and found that Anna had scattered her flowers about David's body, and touched, she herself placed her roses about his head. She remembered the red rose placed just behind her father's right ear to hide the wound where the bullet had entered his head, shattering the greater half of his face and head on the left-hand side at its point of exit. That part of his head and face had been swathed in bandages and somehow it had all looked less horrific than it had really been. She fondled briefly the sparse, greying hair, remembering it had once been the wheaten hue of beaten gold and how striking it had looked when sunstruck. How in dimly lit places, halls or porches or in the village church, it took on a dazzling glow as if by some strange power it attracted and reflected light. She kissed him farewell. First on the forehead and then on one hand which lay on his chest. And finally on the lips. Then briskly she pinned the one perfect rose she had been capable of finding in Mother's overgrown garden where they now ran rife with a vigour and healthy beauty they never attained even under the loving and devoted care of Mr Cowles, who pampered them because Mother loved them and considered them and lily-of-the-valley as being her favourite flowers, on the lapel of his tunic. Steeling herself she turned aside abruptly, swearing not to look at him again. Anna, visibly frightened at the ordeal, went to follow her example. She winced when her lips touched the glacially cold forehead. Gertrude took her by the trembling shoulders and said, "Thank you my love. That's quite enough, you good, brave girl," and gently moved her away, relieving her of further contact with the dead.

She summoned the undertakers and like actors long denied their rightful part on the stage, they entered and took command. At a nod from the man in black — why do I persist in thinking of him as the man in black? Gertrude wondered, they're all in black — they put the lid on the coffin and screwed it down manually with two brass screws, one at either end. They would, she knew, remove them discreetly once they were inside the crematorium building. Its weight seemed to cause them no difficulty. Two of them held it at either end at about waist level — all the better to enable them to control the weight of the coffin and the body within. Following the man in black who went ahead like a grim herald, they moved downstairs in a way that was both slick and professional and elicited at least some slight admiration. The sharp turn at the porch caused a slight difficulty but under the whispered directions of the man in black it was overcome and some seconds later the coffin was slid smoothly into position in the back of the hearse. The engine of a car, one of the long, sleek kind termed 'limousine' which was drawn up behind the hearse, purred into life and continued to do so with smooth content. She stared at it in stupefaction and exchanged glances with Anna, who also looked both puzzled and troubled. The man in black noticed her hesitation and approached, asking, "Is there anything wrong, Madam?" His 'Madam' had progressively taken on a sharper edge since first they had met that morning.

"Yes," said Gertrude, furiously, "there is. I have no intention whatever of getting into that hideous motor . . . It looks like a beetle or worse, a dirty, fat slug. I intend travelling in my own motor."

She ferretted about in her black handbag and finally found the keys to her car. "Wait a moment please. I shan't be long," she said and strode off, her feet crunching the gravel underfoot in undisguised aggression. All the men in black exchanged glances of despair. One, the lean, gaunt man who had produced the glass of water for Gertrude when she had her attack of hiccups, smiled, his lips curling in contempt. The man in black turned his eyes towards heaven and swore violently under his breath. The third man glared at Anna as though she were responsible for the whole delay. Then, whether absentmindedly or deliberately, he turned aside and spat lightly, grinding the spittle into the gravel. He ground it heavily, displacing the pebbles to some depth showing the damp pebbles farther down which testified to the recent showers of rain. Then he stared at her again as though she was someone of malign intent.

Gertrude appeared in her minute, pre-war motor and crunched in upon the gravelled area before the house. She opened the door and Anna climbed in beside her. Gertrude rolled down the window on her side and beckoned to the man in black who by now was clearly the senior representative of the firm of undertakers. "You pull out," she directed bluntly, "and send that filthy monster home and the men with it."

"But Madam," the man protested archly, "I shall need the assistance of at least one of my mate . . .," he was halfway through the word before he hesitated and corrected himself, ". . . one of my colleagues to help me with the remains."

"Don't use that phrase," Gertrude snapped. "Call it by its proper name . . . the body." The man swallowed hard and appeared to be about to say something possibly rash, and thinking better of it, chewed on his words. "Very well," Gertrude agreed, "take one with you in the hearse. Send home that sallow-faced fellow with that filthy black slug. I've never seen such a hideous monstrosity in all my life." The man swallowed hard again and this time touched the brim of his cap. "Yes Madam." Gertrude concluded her spate of bad-tempered directives. "I'll pull in behind the hearse in exactly two seconds. In three seconds I expect us to be under way."

The man in black nodded his head in agreement. He crunched his way to where his companions were waiting by the hearse like shawled women gossiping. There was a pause and what appeared to be crisp, effective speech on the part of the man in black. The sallow-faced man who had stared so offensively at Anna now glared at her in open hostility. He climbed into the sleek car and, unduly harshly, spun it out of position behind the hearse and continued on down the drive until it was lost from sight. The man in black took his remaining colleague by the arm and led him directly to the driver's side of the hearse. The man climbed in and in seconds the motor was running smoothly. The driver hooted his horn quietly to signal preparedness and Gertrude did the same, realising with a pain about the heart that they had gone through exactly the same ritual with a different firm of undertakers during her father's funeral. Poor Father, she thought. I rarely think of you now. I cannot recall your voice . . . though I can Mother's. I can hardly recall your face in any great detail and my memories of you have grown ever dimmer despite the acute sense of treachery accompanying the unconscious, the unwilled, betrayal. They moved off and she was hardly aware of the fact that she was driving a car. I expect it will be in time the same with David. Come to think of it I expect it will be true of myself. Who is there left to remember me? Somehow in a way which was odd and pathetic and even, she felt, shameful, she did want to be remembered. A little. If only a little. Anna, she thought as they passed through the gates, Anna will always remember me in varying degrees of fidedity . . . Should she, Gertrude, pre-decease her . . . For her part she felt she would remember Anna to the day of her death. Nobody, she thought, will ever associate us with the house. The dear old place which had been so full of life and despite some tragedy, jollity and happiness . . . I'll inscribe all their names with a diamond on

a window pane on the landing . . . just where the stairs divide
and where Mother always placed her most beautiful flowers,
her most striking creations. That way they will from time to
time be recalled, if not in pity, at least in curiosity. Perhaps,
she continued to think, perhaps I could endow a memorial
fund of some kind. Cancer research . . . heart disease . . .
something humanitarian, something practical like that. That
is, she reminded herself grimly, if there was any money left
worth mentioning. Which she doubted.

They were out in the open countryside meandering through
roads tall with hedgerows and banks wild with flowers and
high sedges. As they proceeded a cold, clammy dread began
to grow. They were, she realised, swiftly approaching the
point of departure. In a quarter of an hour or so it would all
be over. David would be gone forever and all material traces
of him virtually obliterated. She felt nausea rise and regretted
not having eaten at least a little food. Anna coughed slightly.
The hearse in front signalled caution and paused a few
moments. She did likewise and in a matter of seconds she
followed the hearse onto the main road. Only when they
were within minutes of the crematorium did it strike her
forcibly that she had as her sole companion a Jewish girl
whose all known relatives had, as far as could be established
with certainty, perished in a concentration camp of one kind
or another.

"Anna," she asked quietly when the crematorium came
into view, a cluster of Italianate, redbricked buildings some-
what in the style of a Franciscan foundation, with a sham
belfry which was in reality the chimney tower. "Anna," she
repeated, "you don't mind coming with me? You don't mind
being here?" Even as she asked the question she remembered
the screams as Anna relived in her dreams the horrors of the
camps as exposed by the newspapers after the end of the war.
Anna looked at her frankly, faintly accusatively. "I don't
mind at all. It's just a flash of intense heat and it is all over
. . . It's why they are cremated that matters."

The hearse glided to a halt and even before it stopped the
man in black was out of the front seat and sliding out of the
hearse. A figure in black, fat and with all the fleshy content-
ment of an eunuch, approached her as she and Anna got out

of their car. He smiled broadly and unbefittingly and said, "Mrs Gaunt," and took her hand and shook it, tightening his grasp to convey sincerity, oblivious of the fact that Gertrude had no wish whatever to have her hand shaken. "Miss Gaunt," she corrected him and then wondered why she could be so stupid about observing the social niceties at such a time and in such a place. The man inclined his head slightly in apology but did not in fact apologise or correct himself. He entered the building ushering them, or more properly, shepherded Gertrude and in passing through the small, foyer-like antechamber, he expertly extended a hand behind his back, flicked down a switch and instantly organ music sounded all about them, sad and sombre. Following behind, Anna had seen what the man had done but the man, now priest-like as though to order, had dismissed her as being a person of little or no importance. They entered the interior of the church-like building now suitably adapted for the reception of an atheist, which meant the absence of all religious symbols and a profusion of flowers instead and heard the opening strains of 'Jesu, Joy of Man's Desire,' and as the choir began the accompanying chant she wondered what the fat man thought of her insistence that there should be no religious symbols whatever to be seen during the ceremony and yet insisted on a Christian hymn to begin the brief service. David sang but not well. And this was his favourite hymn, a number of which he knew and which he was liable to sing when in the best of humours with a gusto and force not usually associated with hymns. The coffin was borne in solemnly by four men. Again Gertrude was struck by the thought that it could not be very heavy since David in life was so greatly reduced by illness . . . death had all but plundered what remained. They slowly approached the dais before a curtained alcove. Reaching the dais they placed the coffin on it in a series of moves executed with military precision. They then stood stiffly at attention while they waited for the cantata to end. The sleek, pampered-looking man with his great surplus of fat which showed in his great girth and the many folds of flesh, and whose jowls hung repulsively like an old woman's breasts, stared at them both, his small, deeply set eyes of curious neutral grey, and shot Gertrude a glance as the music ended and its last note lingered on. The phrase, "After sung song, unsung silence," echoed in Gertrude's mind. It didn't make very much sense but she found herself believing that this is how she would remember the ceremony. As if saddened by his role of inter-denominational preacher denied him, the fat man, his eyes registering self-indulgent betrayal, nodded to the men by the dais. They stepped backwards and were no longer visible. The man again nodded. There was the distinct sound of a ratchet slipping into place. A low hum and the dais began to move slowly towards the curtains at the back. There sounded the first notes of Handel's 'Largo' and Gertrude watched with fascinated horror as the dais moved to the curtains, now parted to receive it and the coffin. She found herself being wrenched in a manner she would have thought impossible. A wrench she had felt when, with a soft sigh, David had died. Then she had been hurt to the core but accompanying the wound was a sense of relief. Relief and in a way a sad delight, that thirty years after the cessation of hostilities David had taken his place amongst those remembered annually with vividly scarlet poppies, many prayers and intonations and at the eleventh hour of the eleventh day of the eleventh month, silence. Now, as the curtains closed behind the dais and the coffin on it, she felt impelled forward and thought to rise to her feet. Anna laid a restraining hand on her arm and resumed her seat, whispering, "Goodbye my love, Goodbye dear David." The notes of the music soared higher and higher and in her mind became a splendid white bird which dared to brave the very sun itself and whose wonderful body with its marvellous wings, brilliantly white and spanning quite two foot, hovered momentarily and were tipped with a radiant whiteness ... the whiteness of a high summer sun. It executed, as if in homage, a series of exacting movements and then was absorbed by the sun, the consuming source of all light and life. There was a faint humming sound and she knew the bright, searing flame was consuming David. She worshipped that white, clean flame as against the filth of decay-inducing earth. She worshipped the flame. Then, just then ... when it reduced David's mortal remains to white ash, she wept, and so did Anna. The music ended and there was silence. A palpable silence which no one dared disturb knowing that, according to convention, Gertrude and Gertrude alone could break it. Realising as much she coughed and rose and, unaccountably, inclined her head in a restrained bow towards the hanging curtains of deep purple and then tip-toed from the building as from a church.

The fat man greeted her and brought her to a seat in the Garden of Remembrance which was in fact a rose garden at the lowest level of a series of falling levels, each covered in fine stone slabs and with solid teak garden seats and rectangular beds of roses, and left them.

They sat down and, despite a sense of disrespect, Gertrude furrowed about in her handbag for some cigarettes, not that she particularly wanted to smoke but because she felt her hands were awkward and somehow unseemly and she wanted to use them. There were none there. She had left Mrs Platt's packet behind her in the house. She swore silently in aggravation and then thought, without any pain, I died a little back there. A part, in infinitesimal part, but important for all that. Anna sought her hand and she took it gratefully. They sat in silence.

The man in black approached rather uncertainly and whispered, "A cigarette, Madam?" She nodded and he whisked out a silver case and flicking it open offered her a selection of brands. She silently admired the sheer professionalism of it all and helped herself. The man obligingly lit it for her from a silver lighter with a solitary diamond set in its centre which glinted coldly when caught by the sunlight. She liked him, she decided, smiling her gratitude, despite all his niggardly faults. She had after all been rather difficult about the whole matter and he had tried to do what must basically be an unpleasant task. Then while she was still lighting the cigarette from the flame of the lighter, he slipped a hand inside his pocket and took a neatly folded handkerchief, perfectly white and unused, which he unfolded to reveal David's ring of blue and gold. "The ring, Madam. I forgot to give it to you at the house." He laid it on the palm of her extended hand. The blue shimmered and seemed to ripple in the sun. The gold positively blazed. She said "Thank you" to the man, who then withdrew, and taking Anna's hand she pressed

the ring into the palm and closed her fingers tightly over it.
"I want you to have it . . . as a memento of David . . . and of
me," she added, wondering why she had done so.

Anna nodded and clasped the ring to her breast and quite
unconsciously she struck her breast three times and her lips,
as if in silent prayer. "I shall keep it," she said, "always."

"It won't fit my love, I'm afraid," Gertrude whispered,
"But you can wear it on a chain around your neck, though
that might hurt. Perhaps we could have it refashioned as a
brooch later on." Anna nodded assent. Gertrude glanced at
the deeply blue sky with only wisps of clouds visible far to
the east. She felt a school-holiday sense of pleasure fill her
and wondered why and realised that unconsciously she was
glad that it was David and not she herself who had died.
Lurking at the back of her mind was a certain glee at her
survival. Her time would come, she knew, but there was a
satisfaction in knowing it had not yet come. Such, she
thought, is the constancy of the human heart.

The fat man she so distinctly disliked came down the
flight of steps to the lower garden. Behind him followed
another man in black. Thin and weedy, looking like someone
who existed on a starvation diet. He carried as he might carry
the Holy Grail, a bronze urn containing David's ashes.

The fat man inclined his head. "Had the deceased any pre-
ference in roses and their colour?"

Gertrude shook her head. "Not that I can recall."

"Then you yourself perhaps have a decided preference?"
the man persisted gently, his tone implying only the deranged
could have possibly failed to consider and resolve the matter.

"Red I think . . . yes, red rather than scarlet or pink.
Certainly not white or yellow."

The man beamed. "Then red it shall be." He gestured her
towards a bed of roses with a fleshy hand with short, thick
fingers. Surprisingly, she noted, he wore no rings. She would
have thought him the kind who relished many gaudy, expen-
sive rings. They approached a bed of roses closely planted
and creating an impression of a roll of brilliant red, like a bolt
of the finest silk carelessly slung the length of the bed.

"Would you rather I attended to . . . ?"

Gertrude nodded.

The man carefully removed the lid from the urn and scatter-
ed the ashes amongst the mulch and some soil recently
exposed at the roots of a bush. There are, thought Getrude,
worse destinies than this. Less splendid resting-places than
amongst the roots of a rose bush brilliant with flowers in
bloom. The task done the man replaced the lid on the urn
and returned it to the thin man who hovered about, distaste-
ful subservience in his every move.

Gertrude simply said, "Thank you," and wondered why
the man aroused such repugnance in her, and then turned to
go.

"One moment Madam, please."

She turned frowning to face the man.

He had a miniature pair of gold scissors in his right hand.
"Perhaps I may be permitted to offer you a token of remem-
brance?" He indicated the bed of roses.

"Yes, I should like that," Gertrude replied and thought
how very kind he was. It could hardly be a stock-in-trade
gesture. To do so after every scattering of ashes would denude
the bushes in a matter of days.

He expertly cut a fine flower without once endangering
the scattered ashes beneath, and gave it to her. She took it,
again thanked him sincerely, feeling great gratitude for so
thoughtful a gesture and wondered why she still so heartily
disliked the man.

As they left, Gertrude extended her hand to the fat man
who took it in his with unexpected gentleness and shook it
with considerate lightness. All who felt they should bow,
bowed, and they had soon regained the privacy of the car.
The man in black came towards them. She rolled down the
window with some annoyance. "I don't want to alarm you,
Madam, but our establishment is just a few miles back up
the road. Would you rather go first?"

"Yes, I think I'd rather go ahead," she replied more tartly
than she intended or the man's consideration warranted.
"I've enough of hearses and fat, ugly, sluggish cars for one
day. But thank you for asking me. I do appreciate your kind-
ness. Believe me."

The man tipped his peaked cap and withdrew.

"Thank you, Madam."

*

Gertrude swore mildly. "Damn it, this leatherette is scorching from the sun. It almost burns." She finished her cigarette and ground the stub to pieces in the ashtray in the dashboard. Suddenly she was hungry. "I'm dying with the hunger," she said bluntly, "Could you manage some food?"

"Yes," Anna said shortly but not with conviction.

"Good," said Gertrude, "We'll find a decent hotel and make pigs of ourselves. No use in raiding Mrs Platt's larder. There's probably damn all in it."

She turned the car in the forecourt of the crematorium and, seeing her way clear, began to inch her way onto the main road. Spotting a break in the oncoming traffic she pulled out smartly and turned to regain the correct side of the road. As she did so a car travelling at high speed turned the bend behind her. Before they knew what was happening they were struck side on and the car was thrown back across the road. Gertrude's head flopped awkwardly. A slight trickle of blood issued from her mouth and then just as Anna realised that Gertrude was dead, she found that she herself was pinned in the upturned car. There was a strong smell of petrol. There was a great explosion. Flames engulfed her in a matter of seconds.

Part III

Part III

· ANNA

She arrived at the isolated station as the sun prepared to set behind the western islands beyond which lay the endless stretches of the Atlantic. The air was soft and mellow. The sky was streaked with crimson which she knew augured well for the morrow. In her heart she was humbly grateful. The journey across the country from the city had been slow and tedious. The trip had not been without incident.

A group of foreign students, male and female from one or other of the Scandinavian countries, had shared her carriage on the crowded train. They had made her the butt of their humour. She did not know what they said but one youth in particular, handsome and with the arrogance of those to whom even at an early age sexual conquest comes easily, had been her chief tormentor. He carried out a running commentary on and about her which induced in his companions gusts of laughter which had she heard under other circumstances, she would have felt compelled to describe as happy and carefree.

She had sought to ignore them and nibbled timidly on limp, dry sandwiches and sipped foul tea from a thermos which had sugar and milk already added, and which she had made herself in preparation for the journey, having been informed a dining-car was not always available on the train. She had caught the young man's eye as he seemed about to make further derisive comment. He paused, fell silent and then, as though ashamed, he looked away. He maintained sullen silence for the rest of the journey, failing to respond to his companions' efforts to restore his good humour.

Her arrival at the station had not gone unnoticed. Even as she struggled from the train those crowding about, eager

135

to greet visitors or friends, shrank back as though scorched by flame. They were struck by her ugliness and deformity and though she stood on the platform clutching her small suitcase, obviously needing assistance, no one made an effort to help her. They remained frozen, incapable of even the most elementary courtesy. She stood there uncertain of her next move.

The students alighted with a great deal of laughter. The boy who had sought to humiliate her approached, his companions watching, plainly expecting something outrageously and memorably funny. Oddly solemn and dignified, he held his two hands straight at his side, he stopped some two feet or so from her. He looked her straight in the eye and then he bowed very correctly and stammered in uncertain English. "Forgive me, Madam . . . I have behaved unpardonably." He again bowed and turning walked swiftly away. She very nearly broke at the naked honesty of his admission and realised that it had taken courage to make what had been an act of submission in full sight of his companions. She turned aside and stared intently at the apparently receding rails in the distance.

There was a wild clatter of hooves and wheels as a cart arrived outside the station. A man with wild, grey hair strode onto the platform.

"The curse of Christ crucified on the pack of you. I saw what happened. If she had 'Yank' tattooed all over her, you'd have broken your fucking necks helping her off the train."

The man's obscenity electrified the crowd. Some bristled, most showed embarrasment or discomfort and turning away began to converse in low tones with those nearest them. The man touched the peak of a tweed cap set rakishly at the back of his head. "Murphy, Tim Pat Murphy, Mam . . . but Murphy will do. I'm the man who got the Lauders' place ready for you." He extended a hand to be shaken. She took it with pleasure and thanked him for arriving. "You're very welcome Mam, you're very welcome indeed." She again muttered her thanks. He turned and bellowed to one of the station-porters hovering about, "Have you anything there for this lady, Dinny?" Dinny nodded towards a big trunk which had been hastily taken off the luggage carriage and left at the

far end of the platform. "There's just a trunk," he replied.
"A heavy trunk." The emphasis was on the word heavy. "Ah
now," Murphy taunted savagely. "Are you afraid it has teeth
and will bite the arse off you?" The porter wisely declined
to comment. The last passengers were leaving the platform,
including the young students. They avoided looking at her
but their leader paused, raised a hand in friendly salute and
hurriedly joined his companions. She was struck by the
absence of youth at the station. The students provided a
sharp and telling contrast with the very young, the middle-
aged and the elderly who had gathered to meet the train.

Murphy went down and together with the porter they
hauled her trunk to the cart outside. She followed and was
just in time to see Murphy slip the porter some coinage. He
himself lashed the trunk to the cart with a heavy rope. He
signalled her to approach. She did so with dread, knowing
what must follow. He took her small suitcase and placed
it carefully in the cart. He then addressed her in a voice ob-
viously intended to carry. "Hold your head up, Mam.
Wherever you go and whatevever you do, hold your head up
amongst these people. I know them, seed and breed for gene-
rations past, and if I was to tell you some of the things I
know about them, they'd be screaming to have the very rocks
themselves open to hide them. You're the equal of some," he
added vehemently, "and better than most!" Then more
quietly, he said kindly, "Put your arms to your sides now."
She did so and in one swift movement, he lifted her effort-
lessly onto the right-hand side of the cart. She flushed with
gratitude and pleasure. She had been dreading this moment
all day. They left the station and passed by the small village
huddled about a small quay. Its houses and shops were small
and close together for protection. The two churches were
without steeples. The winters she surmised were most likely
tempestuous and would therefore ensure for her the isolation
she sought so desperately.

The house was a two-storied building with a flat roof and a
crenellated parapet rising above. It looked like a fortress and
stood in stark isolation on an outcropping on the western
side of the headland. To the west lay the western islands,
now dark and distant, and beyond the great waters of the

Atlantic. To the north was a small, smooth beach protected
by the small promontory. Rock formations on either end
effectively sealed it from access except from the rough
ground and sand dunes directly in front of the house. To the
south of the house lay somewhat better land and in a hollow,
scarcely visible amongst the stunted apple trees and thorn
bushes, was an old farmhouse and some stout outbuildings.
As she was to learn later the farmhouse looked deceptively
derelict. There was a harsh grandeur about the place where
earth and sky and water all met, which appealed deeply to
her. She smiled her pleasure. Murphy's eyes sparkled with
delight. He helped her down off the cart. "Faith I was afraid
you would turn tail when you saw the place."

A handsome woman of about thirty stood in the door-
way to welcome her. She was black-haired and upright and
had the striking dignity one sometimes encounters amongst
islanders. She embraced her warmly and said, "Welcome,
Mam. Welcome and God grant you'll be happy amongst us."
The spontaneous embrace, the striking warmth of the welcome
struck her forcefully. She had not been expecting them. She
killed the instinct to weep. "Come inside," the woman said.
"You must be dead with the hunger and tiredness. It's a long
old journey." She took her case from her and ushered her
into a room off the short and narrow hallway. It was a big
room and ran from a window at the front to one at the
back. Her bed was neatly tucked away in a corner opposite
the open fire. An oval table of good polished wood stood in
the middle of the lower half. The table was covered with a
fine linen cloth and was set for a meal. In the centre of the
table stood a commonplace glass vase filled with wild flowers.
She exclaimed in delight, "How very beautiful . . . and how
kind of you to think of them."

The woman nodded her head, pleased that her gesture had
not gone unnoticed. "Sit down, Mam, and I'll bring you in
your meal. You must be starving after all your travelling."
She slipped off her coat. Murphy took it and carefully draped
it on the bed. She sat at the table and to her dismay saw that it
was only laid for one. "Won't you both be joining me?" she
asked, knowing instinctively that they liked her and she in
turn had liked them almost on sight. The woman came

through with a plate of cold meats and salad and a teapot which she set in the centre of the table. "I have a house full of children screaming to be fed and his honour beyond would soon have a puss on him if I didn't go back and feed him . . . him, mark you Mam. Not the children. They could bawl all night so long as his honour had a full belly." She used the term "honour" ironically, yet each time she used it she darted an affectionate glance at him. Only then did she realise that the woman was his wife and not, as she had first thought, his daughter.

She reluctantly sat down to her meal. The woman explained that her son Shawnie would drive out each Saturday to fill her water-barrel from the stream nearby. He would bring whatever provisions were necessary and would collect whatever linen and other clothes needed to be washed and ironed. All this they had agreed upon in her letters to them before renting the house from a London agent. The woman informed her that there was ample turf and some driftwood in the outhouse of the old farmhouse which lay in a hollow to the south of the house and which, though abandoned for many years, had been maintained in good condition by the Lauders, the English family who had originally built the house she was about to occupy, and who had used it as a summer residence during their stay on the island in the happier days of the decade immediately before the war. She also informed her that she was always welcome at their house which lay to the south of the village and if she were lonely, they would arrange with her to stay the night with them. So saying they left, leaving her in possession of the house.

Silence, undisturbed by the murmur of the sea in the background, descended. She felt unutterably weary and old beyond her years. She was as yet only in her mid-twenties yet she looked and moved and sometimes thought of herself as an old woman. She explored the house both out of curiosity and to satisfy herself that all the upstairs rooms were secured and bolted top and bottom and that it was virtually impossible to gain entry to the top of the house without using a great deal of force — sufficient force in fact to wake her should she be sleeping. The exertions necessary to do this took their toll. She considered fleetingly a brief dip in the

sea. It was her firm intention to bathe every day in the sea if
that was at all possible. She had come to this isolated pro-
montory believing that she could draw strength and sus-
tenance from its elemental forces. She decided it would be
unwise to bathe or to try and explore the immediate neigh-
bourhood until she had rested and recovered some of her
vigour.

She tended to the fire and after bathing her right eye
which was subject to continuous discharge and which she
normally kept shaded with an eye-patch, she bolted the doors
back and front and retired for the night. She felt a surge of
despair but the swell of the sea lulled her to sleep. She slept
soundly, dreamlessly, and awoke considerably refreshed. She
experienced acute pain in her hip and the base of her spine as
she always did on waking but she roused herself and drew
back the curtains. Below lay the sea, green-tinted with silver
and here and there ruffled with white. The sands glistened,
sea birds wheeled and swooped everywhere. The islands were
distant, hazed and blue.

She decided impulsively to bathe before breakfast. She
found her bathing gown in a wardrobe in the other big room
off the hallway. Mrs Murphy had unpacked all her clothes
and linens and whatever else she had thought might be neces-
sary to life on the island, all of which she had sent ahead by a
dispatch company. Her linens and underclothing and many of
her frocks had all been carefully washed and ironed and were
neatly stored in the wardrobe or in two chest-of-drawers in
what she now thought of as the storage room. Slipping her
nightdress off she wrapped her robe about her and taking her
bathing cap and a small towel in case she should encounter
someone on the beach and might have to hide her nakedness,
she left the house.

She had difficulty in reaching the beach. The land between
the house and the sand dunes was rough, full of dips and hol-
lows. She stumbled a great deal and on reaching the dunes,
she could progress no farther. She paused in dismay, de-
feated. Then, refusing to yield she threw herself forward and
rolled down a dune. Encountering no broken bottles or razor
shells, she determinedly crawled up the next dune and again
threw herself forward. It was all very painful and in a sense

terrorising, yet she knew that if she allowed herself to be deterred, she could not come to terms with the harsh land and the harsh life it imposed on all who choose to live there. She gained the beach eventually and realised she had won her first victory. It was deserted and she knew access to it was very difficult as the only nearby road was the rough road to her house.

She slipped into the chill waters and gritted her teeth as she submerged her body. She gained sufficient depth where by using her hands stretched back and down behind her, she could float relatively freely. The initial shock passed. The waters were cold but not numbingly so and she knew bathing would be for her an important part of her life in isolation. Satisfied, she left the waters, dried herself roughly with her small towel and, having put on her robe, started back to the house. On her arrival there she found herself so covered with sand, she had to wash herself down again with water from the rain-barrel at the back of the house.

She ate a hearty breakfast and began the task of unpacking the trunk she had brought with her. She had few valuables. What jewellery Gertrude had given her and she had been allowed to keep. Also some photographs of Gertrude herself and of David as a young man, and his portrait which had so delighted her, painted by Mrs Chuckleworth, the vicar's wife. How far away it all seemed. So remote, so distant, so unrelated to her present life, it all seemed like the submerged memory of a previous existence. It was as well, she told herself bitterly. She had won the battle to survive the innumerable operations following the car accident in which Gertrude had died. She won for herself the will to live when she had only sought to die and had in fact attempted to sever her wrists with a piece of broken tumbler. To her surprise one day she woke and found that she wanted to live.

She never accepted the invitation from the Murphys to visit them though Mrs Murphy visited her once or twice. It had been difficult to discourage the gentle and considerate woman from calling too frequently in the false belief that by providing company she was to some extent alleviating her loneliness. Invitations to visit them she quietly but decidedly declined. Only in isolation she felt could she come to terms

with herself and she sought to establish her privacy as soon
and thoroughly as possible. Mrs Murphy did not call again.

The winter passed. Storms were frequent and at first
frightening in their ferocity. The sea crashed on the western
rocks behind the house, the spray on a number of occasions
dashing against the house itself. Its roar was uninterrupted
for days on end. She found it strange and compelling. In a
certain sense frightening but on the whole strangely calm and
invigorating. She didn't bathe on these days. Even the waters
of the small bay were loud and rebellious and strong currents
flowed. She did, however, go to the rock outcrops at the
back of the house and, wrapped in an old cloak which had
once belonged to one of the servants at Scanton, she stayed
for hours watching the thunderous assault of the Atlantic
waters on what seemed to her so small a promontory that
sooner or later it must give way to so sustained an assault.
Her stay on the rocks watching the ceaseless waves as they
broke against the shore with massive force was all the more
invigorating because she knew she was defying the elements.
She had been sternly warned by Murphy against ever ven-
turing onto the rocks even in the finest of weather. The sea
about was subjected to freak waves and some people had
been swept to their deaths in the waters below without the
slightest warning.

On one such visit to the rocks she discovered a gull, its
wing broken and its right leg smashed. It thrashed help-
lessly about on the rocks, crying pitifully. Wrapping her right
hand in successive folds of the heavy cloak, she approached
and despite the fury with which it sought to rip her with its
large beak, she caught and carried it to the house. There she
improvised a nest from an old porter crate and tore shreds of
newspapers to serve until some such time as she could obtain
some straw. She settled the bird in it and covered the top
with some wire mesh which she wrenched from the fallen
fence of the garden below the house.

At first it refused all food but in time it succumbed. It had
been greatly weakened by its injuries and until it was less
wild she could not bind its wing and strut and strap its shat-
tered leg. Gradually it ceased to attack her upon approach.
She fed it a pap of bread and milk and, frequently, raw fish,

chopped into reasonably large portions. Gradually she was able to release it from its cage for short periods each day. It often soiled the place and the house stank of its presence but with the onset of winter she welcomed its company. In time it had the run of the room and she found it satisfied her need for company.

Shawnie Murphy called most Saturdays bringing whatever she needed from the village. She was now less reliant on Mrs Murphy to do all her washing and ironing. She found that she could do a great deal herself with the exception of sheets, blankets and tablecloths. He brought her news from the village and to her amazement she found it interested her not at all. For the first time in many years she was content.

During the long winter evenings, the people of the headland and the village visited each other's houses and the night air was filled with music which could be heard clearly if the wind was sufficiently soft and blowing in the right direction. She opened the door if the weather were fine and, sitting by the fire well wrapped up, the tamed gull in her lap, she listened to the music. Loneliness engulfed her and threatened to overwhelm her. The memory of the dead came to the fore and, at times, possessed her. She longed inexpressibly for the company and warmth and love of another human. She remembered Gertrude, her astonishing beauty, her finely featured face, her beautiful lips and eyes and the pale, slender body with a skin virtually unblemished in any way. She remembered their nights of love and affection and how wonderful it had been to fall asleep in the embrace of one who loved her, and on wakening to find that same lover in the bed. She thought of David, the great love of Gertrude's life, and how she had accepted the primacy of that love and how she had come in time to share it to some extent. She remembered the horror of being informed of Gertrude's death. The distasteful haggle with her distant relatives who had descended on the house with human greed and covetousness rife in their eyes, straining their small, thin mouths as they sought to dispossess her of what Gertrude had sought to give her. But Gertrude had not had the codicil to her will a codicil which was frank and explicit about the true nature of their relationship and which was Gertrude's attestation of

her love for her — Gertrude had not had it witnessed as re-
quired by law and yet, fearing that she might compel them
to give that which Gertrude had clearly sought to give, they
allowed her a small annual allowance paid through a London
solicitor, and some trinkets of moderate value and others
quite without any value other than she loved them or they re-
minded her of her love for Gertrude and Gertrude's love of
her. The old watercolour done by Mrs Chuckleworth, some
photographs, some items of clothing, including some of the
frocks Gertrude had worn with such elegance and which she
in her dementia had hoped she might adapt to her measure-
ments and wear with a similar distinction. She had recognised
her folly and laid them aside. The only visible reminder of
Scanton and Gertrude was a blazing sunburst of monstrance
glory, worked in heavy untarnished gold thread on a back-
ground of heavy, rich, black silk, the possible remnants of a
tapestry or a dressing-gown of great value and beauty of which
only the back panel survived and which she had had attached
to an old screen which she had found in the storage room of
the house. It stood by her bed now and on fine evenings when
the sun shone it struck the screen and the sunburst blazed
with all its intended magnificence.

Possed so of the past, cradling the gull, she was driven
to leave the house and under a night sky of impacted stars to
walk the silver strand which glittered in the starlight, hearing,
hearing with acute pain and misery, the songs and cries of
merriment and the frequently sullen swell of the waters. At
such times, she felt devoid of the capacity to ever love or
trust again emotionally, still less physically. She found the
presence of the gull close to her breast, warm and satisfying
and to some extent fulfilling. Sometimes when the last notes
of music and song had been stilled and the shouted exchange
of farewells had died on the sharp night air, she retired to
the bed cradling the bird to her naked body, fondling its
warm beating breast until she could fall asleep.

On one of her trips to the headland she took the bird with
her cradled safely in her arms. As she watched the calm sea
roll gently, she grew careless. She relaxed her grip on the
bird. In an instant it had leapt from her arms and with a
raucous cry tried to take flight. Its cries alerted other gulls.

Suddenly before she realised what was happening they were swooping in from every side. They relentlessly attacked the bird, pulling it to pieces and devouring it before her very eyes. Their cries had become high pitched, frightening and utterly abandoned. They then turned on her. They dived at her and she fended them off with her cloak. Finally she managed to grasp a sizeable bit of driftwood and beat them off. Stunned and weak both from fright and exertion, she returned to the house and taking some sleeping tablets she made a mug of tea and sat by the fire, a heavy overcoat about her shoulders. She had exceeded the normal dosage and had done so often in the past when she found things unbearable or her hip pained her to such a degree she could no longer tolerate it. Usually she slept soundly and woke in a matter of seventy-two hours and after an initial period of depression she found that she could resume her normal routine to some extent refreshed by her long sleep. Feeling drowsy, she carefully covered the fire with ash, placed the fireguard in front of it and slipped home the safety-catch on either side. She retired to bed and in a matter of seconds she was sleeping soundly. She woke once or twice, thought she heard incessant rain but told herself she must be dreaming. She woke again to a heavy pounding on her door and demands that she open up. She failed to recognise the voice of those moving about outside and, safe in the knowledge that all the windows and doors of the house were safely barred and bolted, she lapsed into sleep.

When she awoke it was dark. Through a chink in the curtains she could see the headlamps of cars as they moved across the high hills at the foot of the mountain proper which lay some miles to the north and under whose shadow the Atlantic Hotel nestled on a superb golfing green and rougher common pastureland on which fairs were frequently held. She woke, wrapped herself in her dressing-gown and going to one of the windows, carefully unbolted the shutters. The night was dark and had a cold, brittle quality about it. The stars were clear and untwinkling. They rose as if in layer upon layer up and out into the dark regions of space itself. To her astonishment she heard the sound of a dance band quite clearly. There must be a dance at the Atlantic Hotel, she thought, and wondered why they should be having one at such an unseasonable time. She dressed, went out to the kitchen and lighting the range, began to cook a meal. Having done so she decided on impulse to bathe though she knew the waters would be numbingly cold. She took her towel and robe and slipped on her bathing cap, leaving the food in the oven.

She left the house and glanced northwards. The site of the hotel could be deduced by an aura of light which hung over it. The dance music was gay and lively and she suffered momentarily a tinge of envy and bitterness. Reaching the shore she laid her clothes safely above the high-water mark and went forward to the water. It was ice cold. For an instant she doubted her wisdom at bathing at all but continued into the water. The cold water spread underfoot. She shivered but nevertheless continued forward. When the water was knee deep she paused and eased her entire body under, gritting her teeth as she did so. She gave short, hoarse gasps as the stinging coldness enformed her. She lay back and barely afloat, her body drifted to and fro like a trailing growth of seaweed. The stinging coldness passed and she found herself as always enjoying the sense of unimpaired movement submersion in the water aroused in her. She splashed gently, countering the inclination of her body to topple over by thrashing about like a baby seal maintaining its balance with its fins. About her the sea moved making music of its own. She heard it break softly on the shore and soon felt the very rhythm of the waters and its tidal movements. She sought consciously to immerse herself in the source of all life on earth as though by doing so she would rise whole and healed once more by some great grace of nature. Above the stars shone steadily. Occasionally the lights of cars swept the hills on the mainland, their lights brilliantly reflected on the surface of the sea. Once a dog barked. Someone uttered a subdued oath and then the silence, which was heightened by the sound of the sea rather than diminished by it, was once more dominant.

The cold increased, she felt the extremities of her body grow numb. She thought it wise to leave the water but before doing so, she observed what had become a curious ritual and one she knew to be sexual. Seeking the shallows she turned on her stomach and resting the full weight of her body on her hands she moved back and forth rhythmically thrusting at the shifting sands beneath it like a mounted male seeking to burrow deeply into his companion, the object of his desire. Her vagina, so altered by surgery, was nothing but a slight aperture which she could only penetrate with her little finger and then only shallowly, but the clitoris remained unimpaired for arousal and now, as though seeking union with the very sources which stirred the waves, she thrust and thrust and felt raw sexuality assert itself between her thighs. A raw sexuality she knew could never be satisfied as it had been by Gertrude or by the man with the black hair, the very memory of whom aroused deep lust and whose virility and explicit pleasure in the act of love so disturbed her at night when insomnia was rife and the desire for sexual congress was most acute. Quietly, exhausted by her efforts and fearing she might aggravate her body to the point of bleeding as she sometimes did, she lay on the sands just where the advance waves spent themselves by fanning out. She lay at rest, her head with its straggling tufts of hair half-submerged in the waters. She felt the salt water on her lips and thought she could remain here for time and eternity and one day she knew she would commit herself fully to the perpetual waters and she, so fundamentally weak and indeed defeated, would share its strength and so enter into full, irrevocable union. Sometime, she told herself . . . but not yet not just yet.

Christmas came and passed. It was the custom of the neighbourhood and of the islands to put a Christmas candle in the windows to light the Virgin and Saint Joseph on their way to Bethlehem. It was lit to welcome those who had any of their family abroad and who might not be expected for Christmas. Most in the area had sons and daughters in England and some had sons and daughters in America. Emigration from the islands, however, was practically all to America. Their small, neat houses were clearly visible in the moonlight, the candles enticingly beautiful.

Little dark huddles of people could be seen leaving their houses on the island and making their way to the church which was a blaze of light, for midnight Mass. Impulsively, she lit an ordinary candle and placed it in a holder in the

window. Despite the sharp coldness of the night she kept the
door open for some time. She could hear the distinct murmur
of the sea in the background.

Spring advanced into summer. The days lengthened and
she enjoyed the longer evenings, the prolonged twilights. She
still swam. Sometimes she ventured onto the rocks which
shielded her from the full force of the Atlantic. There she
gathered from their sheltered positions small, delicate alpines
of rare beauty. Feeling she was despoiling a fortress of
nature, she placed them in a shallow glass bowl on the table
where they remained to delight her.

*   *   *

She finished bathing and returned to the house.

His shadow cut across the sunlit doorway before she
realised that anyone was approaching. All the blood drained
from her face. She felt her heart constrict in terror.

"Good evening, Mam," he greeted her civilly. "I'm John,"
he added by way of explanation. She stared at him. He was
tall and broad-shouldered, strong and most likely a capable
worker. He had black curly hair of the kind which attracted
her. He had a weather-beaten face and remarkably firm,
white teeth and pink healthy gums. He had a jacket slung
carelessly across his shoulder and carried a bundle which she
surmised contained all his possessions.

She recovered herself, though still feeling sick with fright.
"What can I do for you?" Her voice, she thought, sounded
strained and arched and in a way, very English.

"I was down in the village, Mam, and they thought you
could use a hand about the place in return for some accom-
modation."

She stared at him in amazement. "Are you mad?" she
asked thoughtlessly.

His eyes glittered dangerously. "No Mam, I'm not mad.
Just looking for work . . . Accommodation and work."

"I have no work for you," she replied shortly and very

distinctly. "Or accommodation."

"No Mam. I know you have no work. I was thinking if you left me sleep in the old farmhouse below I'd be prepared to work for you in return. Take in your turf and put in a few drills of potatoes and vegetables. That sort of thing."

She stared at him in confusion. "But I couldn't possibly feed you, much less pay you."

He smiled very charmingly and spoke with infinite patience as one might to a child who was not very bright. "No Mam, you don't understand. I'd work about the headland or the mainland for the best part of the week. Then I'd do what had to be done here. I'd sleep in the old farmhouse below and if needs be I'd feed myself. And if things were good I'd kick in the few shillings rent." He paused and stared fixedly at her. She was aware of the fact that she was being scrutinised in a sexual manner. She found it immensely uncomfortable and, yet, it pleased her in a way she would have difficulty rationalising.

"Did anyone send you?" she asked, suddenly suspicious.

"No Mam. I came of my own accord. I come to the headland this time every year for the planting and stay for saving the turf and bringing in the harvest. I always stay in the house below. At least I have for the last seven or eight years.'

'How did you get in? The place is barred and bolted. Only I have the keys."

"The Lauders stopped coming the few years just before the war. They kept a duplicate set of keys hidden in a thorn bush in case of emergency. I stole them and had a set of duplicates made. Then I returned the Lauders' keys to the bush and when they didn't come for the summer I used the place."

She stared at him dumbfounded. "Didn't the police say anything? Surely they knew you were trespassing on private property?"

"They knew but they didn't mind. They knew no harm would come to the place once I was in it. They knew I was doing no harm whatever.'

A thought occurred to her. "Do you have the keys to this place too?"

"Yes Mam, I have, but I never stayed here."

"Could I have them please? You have no right to them. No right whatever."

He slipped his hand into his pocket and took out a small bunch of keys. He eased three Yale keys off a ring and extended them to her on the palm of his hand. She took them and then as she was about to retract her hand, he caught her by the wrist. She reacted as if stung by the warmth of his touch. His skin was hard from manual work and exposure to the weather. The temperature of his blood was above normal. He held her gently for seconds before releasing her.

"I'm an honest man, Mam, I'll do an honest day's work and I'll keep myself to myself."

He gazed at her, sexuality in his eyes. She stammered in confusion, "I don't know. I really don't know."

He approached her extending a hand slowly and deliberately. He slipped off her bathing cap exposing her head, bald in patches and tufted elsewhere with unruly growths of hair. She whimpered and gently, very gently, he moved the warm palm of his hand about her head as though he was possessed of miraculous powers and could restore her to her former state, unmaimed, unmarked. He touched her lips with the tips of his fingers. Impulsively she kissed them. He slipped off her bathing robe and now with both hands embracing her began to explore what she thought of as her hideous body. He kissed her long and passionately, without restraint. She felt the full force and strength of his body press against her. His warmth and evident desire shocked her beyond measure. She had almost forgotton the warmth of human flesh and the pleasure it afforded. She glimpsed a partially furred tongue, slightly scaled teeth, then his mouth covered hers. His breath was surprisingly fresh and sweet. He bared his teeth and pressing them heavily against her lips, forced her to part. He inserted his tongue into her mouth and explored the roof and under her tongue. He coiled his tongue around hers and she began to experience the assertion of desire as he plucked at her vagina and with his little finger sought entrance. He failed and looked perplexed.

They parted briefly. Puzzled and looking somewhat lost, he stared at her curiously.

She flushed with shame and turned aside. "Please, I've had

an operation. I was in an accident. A car accident. I can't really . . . "

Her voice trailed off and she felt humiliated such as she had never felt before and yet wanting him above all to press close to her so that she might feel again the warmth of his body which penetrated his clothing and his thighs, fuller and warmer than any she had known before, and his powerful upper body which was muscularly hard, hurting when he embraced her too tightly.

"There are more ways of skinning a goat," he said brutally and recommenced his probings, less gently now, more urgently as his arousal became more apparent. She knew he would have her at all costs. He thrust against her. She was forced back against the wall. Her hip and thigh hurt as he pressed heavily against her, pressing her in turn against the wall. She heard him undo his buckle, spit and then, in one controlled movement, he spun her and thrust forward penetrating her anally. She cried out in pain and cried again but he was oblivious of her cries. She felt the undeniable demand of his flesh as, breathing harshly, he sought the correct rhythm for deeper and more effective penetration.

"For fuck sake help," he muttered. "Push down . . . push down."

With an urgency and hunger which surprised her, she thrust down with all her might. The pain was searing but his fulfillment was uppermost in her mind.

He found the rhythm, thrust deeper and deeper and muttered, "Good girl . . . good girl." He climaxed and lay against her back breathing deeply, his two thighs clamped about her grotesquely protruding posterior. She smelt distinctly the pungent scent of excrement, her excrement she realised, and passed him back her small laced handkerchief and its embroidered roses and green stems in all four corners. He muttered his thanks and before she knew what was happening he had slipped off his shirt and lay roughly against her, the full warmth of his body now shaping her maimed body, his two strong but warm hands exploring the front of her body; her thighs, her breasts, the fat folds of her stomach.

There was great tenderness in his touch and he muttered incoherent endearments as one might to a colt or a frightened puppy. Suddenly she wept. The sounds erupted from her mouth as did the tears from her eyes. Why she wept she didn't know. She thought herself long past the stage of weeping. She had wept and screamed and raved in both mental and physical anguish in the years of being confined in a hospital bed while undergoing a series of operations following her rescue from the blazing car in which Gertrude had perished. She had wept bitterly then and very often . . . but not since then.

He stroked her face. "Come on," he said, "there's nothing to cry about." She dried her face with both her hands and they faced each other like strangers, searching one another for, on her part at least, treachery, contempt and, perhaps, affection.

There was an indefinable shyness about him now, a vulnerability she couldn't quite account for but which echoed for her a somewhat similar trait she had found in the black-haired man so many years ago, she couldn't quite remember when . . .

His eyes shone with tenderness and he asked, "Can I wash, Mam?"

"Yes," she replied shortly, struggling into her clothes. "There's water in the rain-barrel around the back of the house. You can take a basin from that and wash on the small table by the mirror there."

The table to the left of the kitchen table at which she ate was small but higher than usual which enabled her to wash without having to bend over too much and strain her painful hip. He nodded his thanks, adjusted his clothing and whistling softly an air of high, clear purity, went outside. She found herself confronted by a sense of inner void, longing desperately for his affection, trust and confidence and for his warm presence, his fit body and his sexual prowess. His sexual demands she knew instinctively were harsher than those of the average male. She knew she would not always satisfy those demands and that he would inevitably turn to others. Nevertheless she wished he would stay.

He came inside still whistling with the basin of water which he laid on the table she used. There was a bar of plain soap to his immediate right. From a cupboard she took a soft towel. She herself used a rather coarse one to stimulate the frozen muscles of her face.

He turned to her and said, "You don't mind, Mam?" He hesitated as she failed to understand. He grinned broadly. "There isn't much between us now."

Suddenly she realised he wanted to strip naked and wash his entire body after his exertions.

"No," she replied rather archly, "I don't mind at all." He smiled and nodded and with a simplicity she found moving he undressed and began to wash his body. She marvelled at his startlingly white skin with only a few blemishes and the lithe muscularity which was visible in his every movement. His hands and face and neck were tanned and weather-beaten in contrast. He caught her scrutinising him hungrily, and laughed. She flushed deeply but he glanced at her and she realised the laughter was pleasant, quite without contempt. It was free and easy, childishly so, and by no means the cavalier laughter of one who had just made an easy conquest. He covered his body with suds in a few deft strokes and then wiped them off with a wet handcloth. He dried himself briskly and stroked his chin as men do when trying to decide if they should shave. He glanced at himself in the mirror. "You don't have such a thing as a razor, Miss?" he asked unhopefully. "I could do with a shave."

"I don't really know. I'll look outside in the kitchen. I think I saw one there sometime. As you know this was used by an English family as a holiday home before the war. Perhaps Mr Lauder left one behind." Her voice faltered and she went into the kitchen. She found a blade together with a worn shaving brush and toothbrushes in a jamjar at the back of a cupboard above the kitchen sink. Littered about it were a number of coiled toothpaste tubes squeezed empty. They struck her fleetingly as being like filthy slugs coiled in upon themselves. There was a mirror on the wall opposite the door. She watched him furtively as he carefully washed his genitals. Then he whistled, holding his head first to the right and then to the left, all the time tapping his chest and upper-stomach with the fingers of his right hand. "I found one but it's rather rusted I'm afraid. I don't think you'll be able to use it." He took if from her and examined it carefully. The blade wedged between the two steel plates was thickly encrusted with rust. He whistled shortly. "I think I can make a fist of it."

He strode to a fireside chair and sitting on it, succeeded with difficulty in separating the plates. He also had difficulty in separating the blade from one of the plates to which it had stuck. He held the blade aloft. "You can't use that," she protested. "It's lethal. It will give you blood poisoning."

"Lethal? That's a big word now. What does it mean?" He cocked his head like an intrigued terrier.

She saw that beneath his levity lurked a bristling sensitivity. He was gifted with an innate intelligence and hid it under a gentle buffoonery. Yet there was something stark and primitive about him. Something elemental and ungovernable, if not deadly.

She looked at him steadily and spoke steadily. "You know perfectly well what it means. You're no fool."

He grinned and nodded his head. "You might be right there. You might be right. Would you have a knife now, Mam, and a box of matches?"

The knife she took from a drawer in the dresser, the box of matches from a bundle of boxes on the mantlepiece. "My name is Anna," she said. "Please call me Anna."

"Anna," he said quizzically, never taking his eyes from the razor which he began to scrape clean with the knife. "That's a fine name. A beautiful name." He paused and pondered as if reaching a decision of some importance to him. "I'll call you Anna," he said slowly. There was a silence broken only by the sound of scraping which set her teeth on edge. "And," he said with that same slow deliberation, "I'm John."

She knew it to be untrue but smiled nevertheless. "John. I rather like it as a name. I always have in fact." Her face was gross, undeniably ugly, and a sightless left eye made her appear more hideous. When emotionally aroused her features were even uglier. Was he not repelled by her? He succeeded in scraping most of the rust off the blade. Patiently he struck a match and holding the blade aloft he drew the flame carefully along the edge of the blade. He's sterilizing it, she thought, and very effectively too. The match burnt out. He dropped it and spitting on the fingers of his left hand, he drew them along the blade. He rose and padding to the fire, scraped each edge of the blade on the hearth stone. He finished and, rising, held up the blade. A thin edge of sharpened steel was visible. "That should do the job." Briskly he inserted the blade in the razor and began to shave.

Darkness was setting in steadily. The sun had gone down and a dim, grey light flooded the room. She hovered about uncertainly. "It's getting dark," she said as though to herself. "Do you think I should light the lamp?"

He nodded agreement. With her usual care which verged on the devout, she drew the table lamp from the centre of the large, round table at the far end of the room and left it within easy reach. She pulled on the thick woollen cap which she wore to hide her partial baldness and went outside with a narrow-lipped jug. She filled it carefully from one of the gallon tins of paraffin carefully stored in one of the well-constructed stone outhouses of the old farmhouse in the hollow farther south. Returning to the house she filled the lamp and, leaving it unlit, she took a smaller metal lamp from its nail beside the fireplace, the one which usually served as her main supply of light at night, and filled it too. She carefully returned the jug to its proper place by the kitchen range. Her every movement was being watched carefully. Tremulously she struck a match and lit each lamp in turn, carefully replacing the glass chimneys. She realised that he couldn't possibly know what terror such a simple undertaking held for her. How each time she lit a lamp or even struck a match, she had to actively obliterate a rising sense of fear, a temptation to scream, by a determined act of the will to see the task through. She replaced the large lamp in the centre of the round table and replaced the small lamp on its nail on the wall. The embroidered rose on its black backing material tacked to the screen shone brightly and seemed to sparkle. There was, she felt, an almost festive appearance about the room and, almost irrationally, about herself.

He continued to shave in silence.

"Would you care for some food . . . something to eat? There's some corned beef and mashed potatoes left over from yesterday. And some cabbage I think." She laughed shortly. "At least I hope there is." Her voice faltered and she flushed at the sheer beggary in her voice. "Perhaps I could fry them for you or," she hastened on in desperation, "perhaps you'd rather wait until you return from the pub?"

She stared at him, delighting in his sheer physical beauty, the ever-changing interplay of muscle which rippled across his body every time he as much as moved.

He stared at her intently, considering the implications of her question which were plain. He hesitated.

She thought of the long winter nights when she had sat by the fireside, the door open, as she listened to songs and dances coming from one of the houses on the headland or farther out on the islands. Her sense of exile and exclusion had almost been unbearable. She now found she couldn't care what the villagers or anyone might think. He'd be company, she thought, if only for a while. There was no one else on the face of the earth who would as much as glance at her a second time, other than in rank curiosity or perverse amusement.

"I think," he said softly, "I'd prefer to wait until after I've had the few drinks. The few drinks will whet my appetite."

She smiled and nodded her head. "I'll make up a bed in the farmhouse below. It's perfectly habitable. The children of the English family who used to stay here before the war had some repairs carried out. There's a good concrete floor with straw matting . . .and there are plenty of bunks there. It isn't in the slightest bit damp. I'll air some clothes for you while you're away and make up a bed for you." She paused, realising she was rattling on hurriedly, almost hysterically. "Of course," she said lamely, "you know all about the farmhouse. I mean you've slept there before."

"I have indeed."

He smiled pleasantly and she smiled also. She was happy for the first time in many years.

He began to dress. From his rucksack he took a white shirt, carefully folded. He shook it out and put it on, and after dressing spent some minutes before the mirror in the kitchen combing his hair. He slipped on his jacket. With the candour of the very vain, he asked, "How do I look?"

"You look splendid," she said quietly. "Perfectly splendid."

He laughed, a schoolboyish laugh and touched her lightly on the cheeks . . . "Well I'll do for now." He glanced at the fireplace. "You'd best be lighting the fire. It's getting cold." He put his hand to the latch and opened the door. "Those are good apple trees out there,' he said casually. "A bit of pruning would do them no harm. The weeds and wild grass around them would have to be dug out and the good heap of manure worked in around them. That bit of ground would make a great potato patch. Man, you could do things with this place if you had a mind to." He smiled winningly at her. He was, she realised, seeking confirmation of her earlier offer.

"Yes," she said. "I imagine you could. But it would take a great deal of work."

"I was never afraid of hard work. Hard work never killed anyone."

"Well," she said, emboldened. "You can always try if you want to." She saw rather than heard her own words as clearly as if they hung suspended in mid-air before her. She found she had to steady herself against the nearest chair.

"I will," he said simply. "I'll have a go . . .and no better man." He smiled, lifted his hand in casual farewell and left. She heard him whistling sweetly as he made his way to the rutted path which led to the road to the village.

She glanced about the kitchen of the old farmhouse. Its timbers were visible and, above, its corrugated iron roof. Its small windows were set deeply into the thick stone wall. A stove in which burned a small, bright fire stood in what used to be the old open fireplace now effectively sealed off. Between two kitchen chairs was slung a mattress. She had positioned it a safe distance from the stove, though the front of the stove had an intact window of mica.

Opposite the door was a tin washbasin in an iron stand. She had laid out a fresh towel on the rack flanking the stand. A mirror hung on the wall above. On a small bedside table she had placed a glazed earthenware ashtray sufficiently large to hold a pipe with safety, and which she had chanced upon some time ago. Above the old kitchen table covered with its oilcloth of pale yellow and its pattern of wildly red cabbage

roses, a wall lamp, its wick freshly trimmed and its oil re-
plenished, shone brightly.

She gazed at the scene and wondered fleetingly if he would
appreciate all her efforts and if the sheets and blankets she
had draped about chairs in her own house would be suf-
ficiently aired before he returned. She turned the lamp low.
He couldn't fail to see it lighting on his return from the
village. She went back to the house. The clothes before the
fire were, she decided, sufficiently aired. They smelt heavily
of mint from leaves she had laid between them while they
were put in storage in the chest-of-drawers. She went to the
open doorway and again listened for possible sounds of mer-
riment or even belligerence which so often signalled the
closing of the pubs in the village. It was closing time but that
wouldn't worry the publicans a great deal. As likely as not,
the sergeant himself was in one or other of the pubs and one
of the guards in another. If a game of cards had started or
there was good music available they would stay there until
the early hours of the morning.

Dawn infiltrated the room through a chink in the curtain
of the window facing the bay. The first advancing light was
faintly blue. She drifted back to sleep and woke later in the
morning to a feeling of sensual delight and momentarily
thought herself back at Gertrude's with the all-pervasive
presence of David who slept on and on imposing his tyranny
of love.

She blinked as she found herself surrounded by the more
familiar things of her room and she heard the sounds of the
sea in the distance. She was puzzled remembering the events
of the last few weeks and then she realised with joy that for
the first time in many years she had woken without the acute
sense of pain riddling her body as it had done since she was
in hospital. Although the pain was still present it failed to
hurt as it had. It was in some remarkable way annulled or
anaesthetised. She heard more clearly the sea lapping against
the shore, the cry of the gulls and other birds she couldn't
identify definitely even on sight. Then she heard it, soft and
distinct, the door of the outhouse opening and the snatch of
a whistled song which announced his rising every morning.
He would, she knew, first piss steadily outside the front

door of the outhouse with little care for the sense of modesty of anyone who might be passing. She had stolen from her bed to observe his first movements on arising not long after he had settled into the farmhouse and had been thrilled by the sheer, animal vitality he displayed in all his movements.

She rose, grateful for his presence, and slipping on her slippers and dressing-gown went out to the kitchen and lit the fire he had laid the night before. He had undertaken a number of tasks about the house without being asked. He gathered kindling and scoured the strand for driftwood though there was an ample supply of wood in the shed to the side of the house. These logs he cut into more manageable lengths every morning in what was to become a daily ritual for him. He obtained some casual work in one of the pubs in town and accepted in part-payment two barrels which had not been used to contain porter and, having sluiced them thoroughly with scalding water, he set them up behind the house and kept them topped up with fresh water from a well farther down the road. As a result, she was never without fresh water. He himself fetched the provisions from the village. There was therefore no further need for Shawnie to call.

He was now much in demand in the village or about the headland. He was a good and honest worker, handy with his hands, willing to try anything and in most cases succeeding. He took infinite pains to do his job not just well but as superbly as possible. A shrewd bargainer, he knew that money was scarce and what little the farmers had they tended to hoard. He therefore struck a bargain by which he took goods or produce in part-payment. Hence he assured a steady supply of potatoes and vegetables, wood for the fire and turf also, and occasionally part of a flitch of bacon. He sometimes worked in advance for produce to be supplied when in season.

By now she knew he had positioned a flaked mirror on the outside ledge of the window to the right of the doorway and had begun to shave in cold water with his cut-throat razor, his broad back and upper body bare to the elements.

His presence in the outhouse had caused widespread comment in the village and in the neighbourhood. He disarmed their malice by his charm which was considerable once

he choose to exercise it. The others, afraid to confront him
or to be reported as commenting adversely, were silenced
if only because they feared him or needed him as a capable
labourer.

She feared the reaction of the parish priest, a squat, bul-
lying man, who had once preached against a young German
couple who had camped by the village and who had been
known to swim and sunbathe naked. He had forced the shop-
keepers and farmers to stop supplying them by insisting that
by providing them with their necessities they were partici-
pating in what he termed to be grossly sinful behaviour,
offensive to God and the Blessed Virgin. His parishioners
had had no alternative but to comply with his wishes on the
matter. Consequently the young couple were forced to leave
the district. She feared the priest might preach against them,
but inexplicably he had failed to do so. John, she knew, had
attended Mass each Sunday and frequently fasted from mid-
night on the Saturday before receiving communion on the
following Sunday. He had ceased taking communion and
never explained why. She suspected he had been refused it.
He did, however, still attend weekly Mass.

She made some tea and, when drawn, poured a mugful
and added milk and sugar in plenty. Outside there was a
slight drizzle and everywhere droplets of rain hung like
heavy morning dew from the spikes of grass and reed. En-
tering the house she found him sitting on the bed smoking
contentedly, his upper-body bare, waiting for her.

He nodded briefly as she entered. She still felt too shy to
greet him formally. As always she was struck by the neat-
ness and tidiness of the kitchen. His bed was perfectly made.
His razor, brush and soap were all laid out neatly on the
ledge of the window nearest the door. The strop hung near-
by. There was a freshness about the place which always
pleased her. She had found to her surprise — though upon
reflection she failed to see why it should have surprised her
— that in everything he did he tended towards cleanliness
rather than squalor. She handed him his mug of tea and he
lit a cigarette to smoke while sipping it. He gestured her
silently to sit on the bed by him. She did so, her hands
almost primly crossed on her lap. It was perhaps the most

intimate part of their day. They spoke little, if at all, yet
both were acutely aware of one another's presence as if
their bodies had been greatly sensitized. He lay aside his mug
and his cigarette. Unbuckling his belt he lay in on the bed
and drew her with him.

He squeezed her playfully about the waist. He slipped off
her woollen cap and gently stroked her head. It never failed
to rouse him. She kissed him on the lips and then her mouth
sought his nipples. His upper-body was tanned and browned
from his months of work saving turf and hay. He had labour-
ed long and hard and had been handsomely paid. They could
look forward to a comfortable winter and spring and expect
to suffer no great hardship. His earnings in money or kind
greatly enhanced her small allowance. He slipped down his
clothing. From the lush growth at his groin hair spread up
his body and divided towards each nipple like a dark, pal-
maceous growth. Quietly she lay her head on his chest, her
ear in close, deliberate contact with his breast in order to
hear the stout rhythm of his heart which beat strongly,
soundly, resonantly. Enthralled, she gently roused him with
her finger tips, gently tugging at his pubic hair. He responded
rapidly. She slipped off her dress and crawled upon him,
straddling his body, allowing the full weight of her's to lie on
his. She explored his mouth with her tongue and he roughly
stimulated her buttocks and the base of her spine. His heart
beat more rapidly. Urgently he forced her face towards his
thighs. She kissed his breast, his stomach, the erect penis,
then experiencing an almost instinctive hunger she took
it in her mouth. He groaned and his body shifted. His
pleasure she knew was intense and she felt grateful that
she could satisfy him to such an extent. She drew hungrily
on him as if feasting on what his body would yield, strength,
stamina, resilience. Her hunger was manifest and much
greater than that of any infant feeding at the breast. He
groaned, his body arched. He climaxed. She lay still, her head
resting on his groin, his now limp member still in her mouth.
He stroked her head affectionately. "You're a whore for it,"
he said lovingly. "A terrible whore altogether." He shifted his
body and began to readjust his clothing. She smiled at his
comment and pulling on her cap, told him to hasten or he

would be late for breakfast and hence for work. He struck her affectionately on the rump.

He loves me, she thought as she passed up to the house . . . in his way. As for me, I love him more than I can possibly say or even thought possible and I shall never be able to tell him.

What they termed 'Amusements' had been erected on the green in front of the Atlantic Hotel. For the greater part of two days heavily laden lorries had moved up the road from the village. They did not pass very close to the house so they really hadn't impinged upon her. Now, however, they had succeeded in erecting some of the amusements, chair-o-planes, dodgem cars and swinging boats and wished their presence to be known to the entire headland and the outlying districts. All day she had to listen to the wailing voices of singers singing the most popular songs of the day from blaring loud speakers. To her dismay they were for the most part raucous rather than melodious, of love lost, rather than of love gained. They aroused in her a deep melancholy which deepened as the day progressed. She did little work about the house. Her thoughts kept returning to Gertrude and David and their memory hung heavily on her mind. She so rarely thought of them now. She had forced herself to cut the stream of memory as though it were a flowing ribbon and turn her attentions elsewhere immediately she caught herself thinking of them, because she knew from experience that if left unchecked they would in time overwhelm her and she would succumb to despair. The evening had a bright, autumnal glow about it. The air was keener and colder. She did not go and bathe, and despite the sky which still retained a great deal of splendid, enticing colour, she huddled by the fire. She felt feeble and debilitated.

He returned and she realised guiltily, and with some fear, that she had forgotten to prepare his food. She stared at him. He touched her gently, infinitely gently, on the face. Inexplicably she wept bitterly on his shoulder. He put her to bed assuring her he would take care of everything. She immediately capitulated to an overwhelming weariness of the spirit which completely undid her. She fell into a deep sleep. Once or twice she woke during the night and to her relief he was there by the fire, seated on a chair, an old overcoat across his shoulders, a blanket about his knees and the fire sufficiently lively to afford some heat. She knew she could count on his presence to see her through the night which she dreaded quite without reason. Shadows danced alarmingly on the walls of the room and in uneasy sleep, she drifted into and out of dreams of her chequered past. Around dawn she woke. He brought her a mug of tea which she barely sipped. He touched her on the forehead and on the cheek and she thought, why is he so sad? She immediately drifted into sleep again. Deep, unbroken, restorative sleep, undisturbed by dreams. When she woke it was close to midday. Sunlight flooded the room. Everything it touched seemed renewed. It struck a jar of wild flowers on her bedside table which hadn't been there the night before. She realised that he must have picked them and placed them in the jar before slipping off to work. She delighted in them and touched them lovingly, sharing briefly in the commonplace glory of the miracle of life, its simple cycle shaven of all the complexities of the troubled mind, the clouded vision, and appearing in sharp definition as a simple, full and fulfilling circle.

Her spirits lightened. She rose, bathed her eyes and sat down to a hearty breakfast. She opened the front door and the upper half of the outer half-door and began the contemplative task of washing the delph, her mind tranquil and at ease. Her day passed in happy abstraction. She set the tea table.

Hardly had she done so when a shadow cut across the irregular pattern of sunlight streaming through the half-door, striking the bare floor. She looked up somewhat startled and felt a chill. A young woman of striking beauty cradling a child in her arms stood there, her bearing almost queenly, her pose that of the classical Madonna. She was perfectly clean in body and clothing. Her hair was black and lustrous and carefully combed. Even her teeth were white and looked as if they received daily attention, something exceptional from what she knew of the people amongst whom she had chosen to live. Her face was placid and calm but there was an alarming glint in her eyes, a coldness which hinted at detached hatred and brutality.

She spoke plainly and evenly, scorning the whining tones of the professional beggar and failing to screw her features into a plastic study of hardship and deprivation.

"Would you have a few coppers, Mam, or the drop of milk for the child?"

She stood staring at the woman, shivered again and said, "Yes, I can give you some money. But only a little. I have very little for myself." She went to the mantlepiece where she stacked her odd coppers. She turned and gave them to the woman who scarcely glanced at them before enfolding them in her fist and then stared at her intently.

She found herself apologising for the closed half-door. "I'm sorry I can't open the door but I have a kitten . . . a little kitten and I'm afraid it might stray and get killed on the road." She wondered at her capacity for blatant falsehood. The woman recognised the statement for what it was. A faint smile curled her lower lip, when she spoke her voice was touched with contempt.

"A kitten, Mam?"

"A kitten. A very small, black kitten. It isn't house-trained yet and has no sense of traffic."

The woman nodded. "God bless it but it must be great company and you alone all day."

"Yes, it is great company."

Only when she had spoken did she realise that she had fallen into a trap of her own making. She knew that she was being both scrutinised and interrogated with expert cunning. The woman glanced behind her at the table set for the evening meal. It was set for two. She then turned and gazed at the hollow below the house. The apple trees had been pruned, their lower trunks ringed with lime. The potato drills with their withered stalks and which promised a good crop to anyone with even only an elementary knowledge of husbandry. She glanced at the neatly chopped firewood stacked outside the door and the newly made rick of turf with a canvas spread over its top and expertly pegged, to protect it during the winter.

The woman turned back to her. Her eyes were hard and glinting with unappeasable hatred. Her voice was bitter and had the quality of sharp, cutting steel. "God bless you, Mam, but you have the fine husband. He has the place in great condition altogether."

Stupidly thinking it would hurry the woman on her way she said, "Yes. I'm expecting him home for supper very soon." She immediately saw her mistake. The fact that she wasn't married could easily be determined by casual enquiry in the village at any time.

The woman smiled a bitter, triumphant smile. "It's fine for you entirely," and pausing, stared her straight in the eyes. She looked away, unable to meet the unflinching eyes of the other. For all that there was triumph of a kind to be seen there, a certain sadness had entered them and sadness was detectable in her voice when she spoke.

"God bless you, Mam. . . . You wouldn't have the few clothes or rags itself?" The beggary in her voice was false and automatic, quite untouched with the desperation of the genuine beggar.

"No, I haven't . . . I'm sorry. . . ." She began to close the inner door when the woman nodded and said in quiet simplicity and clarity, "Thank you, Mam, and may God bless you and yours." Turning she walked slowly up the rough path and turned towards the road down to the village without ever once glancing back. Oddly, her parting blessing was not without a certain sincerity and compassion.

She closed the door and was very much afraid for reasons she couldn't understand. She settled down to wait for him. He hadn't come by his usual suppertime. Several times she rose from her place by the fire and went to the door to listen for the whistling which invariably signalled his return. The monotonous music of the roundabout began and carried far on the sharpening evening air. She closed the door and sat by the fire. To the west the sun sank beneath the waves behind the western islands. That part of the room which faced westwards was bathed in a light which was almost unearthily beautiful and which almost always delighted her. She toyed with the poker in her ever increasing anxiety, jabbing the burning wood and peat, causing them to spark. Finally she could wait no longer for his return before bathing. Dusk was already falling.

She took her bathing-gown and with the usual difficulty made her way to the beach. The first few stars were clear against a sky of muted blue fading into darkness. Already some of the cottages on the mainland showed lights. Not until she had stripped and waded into what she considered her depth did she sense that she was not alone.

On the dunes some figures were squatting, all but lost in the oncoming darkness. She estimated there were at least three there, youths or young men. The faint glow of cigarette tips which flared into minute heads of bright pink whenever they were inhaled, glowed distinctly. Whoever was watching felt in no way compelled to keep their presence unknown. Nor had they made any real effort to conceal themselves. She felt instinctively they were not louts from the village come to gape. There had been no difficulty from the villagers or anyone else about her bathing in the past. They would, she felt, hardly concern themselves now.

She pretended ignorance of their presence and affecting a nonchalance she was far from feeling, she thrashed about for some seconds. It occurred to her that they might be men from the fairground or tinkers who were collecting on the headland for the horse fair who had heard of her eccentricity and had come to see for themselves. Nevertheless there was something ominous about them. They posed a threat she could in no way formulate. With the force of a blow it struck her that they were connected with the young woman who had called earlier, and all were connected with John.

Abruptly she rose and turned to leave the water. To her horror she found that they had positioned themselves in a semi-circle to prevent her from doing so. She gasped and then instantly regretted having shown concern. She struggled forward as if totally unaware of their presence. She was in the shallows when the first pebble struck her with stinging force on the side of the head. She yelped shortly in pain. Immediately another struck her just above the right ankle. She cried out in pain again. They echoed her cries with harsh, vindictive laughter. Pebbles struck her all over and peppered the waters about her. She retreated. They intensified their attack. The pebbles gave way to stones, some quite sizeable, and it was obviously their intention to drive her out into the deeper waters and the treacherous undercurrents.

She cried out for help but the music from the funfair drowned her cries. Just as she was about to flounder she heard one of the figures on the beach cry out in pain and yell, "Jasus, Petie, don't man. Don't. For the love of God . . . " The cries ended abruptly. She heard a distinct thud as if someone had been hit savagely over the head with a stout stick or something similar. There was a stifled roar of pain and the sound of feet scurrying on wet, smooth sand. And then they were gone.

With great exertion she struck forward but found herself being dragged back into the deeper waters by the undercurrents. She cried out in despair. A figure waded into the water. Convinced it was one of her attackers she screamed, "For God's sake don't." Again the music from the roundabout drowned her cry. A hand grasped her's and she was roughly dragged from the water. Spent and hysterical with fear, she lay panting on the wet beach almost choking on her own sobs and willing herself to draw strength and sustenance from its solidity. She shivered uncontrollably and her teeth chattered as she relived the horror of being swept out to sea. Her rescuer retreated. Seconds later her towel and bathing gown were brought to her and laid at her side. The dark figure she didn't dare address, addressed her solicitously. "Are you alright, Mam?" She replied, "Yes," and added, "please go away."

"I will to be sure," he replied, "but are you alright?" She knew from his voice that he was young and good-natured and possessed strength of both character and body. "I'm alright," she assured him through chattering teeth. "That's good," he said simply. "That's all I wanted to know." He was about to go when she asked impulsively, "Who are you and why are you here?" He stood some distance off drawing heavily on the stub of a cigarette. 'I'm Petie, Mam . . . I'm down with a few ponies to sell at the fair tomorrow." "But what," she persisted, "are you doing here just now?" He paused and considered. "I was passing, Mam, and I saw the commotion." It occured to her that he had excellent eyesight. "Those people," she persisted. "They tried to kill me." He laughed lightly and spoke as one would to an unnecessarily fright-

ened child, "That was just a bit of sport on their part, Mam."
She moaned in despair. "They tried to kill me and you call
it sport." He fell silent and so did she. Against the back-
ground music from the funfair she heard the waves break
gently on the shore. She experienced a rising sense of de-
solation. "John," she cried. "Do you know John?"

He was silent. When he eventually spoke it was to lie.
"No, Mam. I know no John." "You're lying . . ." Suddenly
she erupted into tears. She wept without restraint and un-
ashamedly. He approached her, knelt and drew her already
soaked gown about her. He fumbled in his pockets and with-
drew a packet of cigarettes. He took one, lit it and offered
it to her. "Take a pull out of that. It will do you the power
of good." "Go away," she begged. "Please go away." He
stiffened. His voice was cold. "I will so." Silently he with-
drew.

Suddenly the music of the roundabout ceased. There was
only the muted sound of the seas and faint, murmurous
wind. Above a flight of wild geese passed, desolation in every
movement of their wings, the sound of which aroused in her
poignancy and the heartbreak of a departure she knew to be
final. Water broke upon her and all about her, drenching
her. The music of the roundabout started again. She struggled
to her feet and drawing her wet robe around her and trailing
her towel limply in one hand, she stumbled and tumbled
across the dunes to the house.

She closed the door behind her and bolted it top and
bottom. Then, moving painfully and more conscious of pain
than she had been for a long time, struggled to the back door
and locked and bolted it also. She stripped herself of her wet
robe, washed her body with a handcloth dipped in tepid
water and dried her hair. She made a pot of tea, slipped on
a flannel nightgown and draping a blanket about her
shoulders and one about her knees, she sipped her tea re-
flectively before the fire. She dozed and eventually nodded
off to sleep feeling that she had been in some way defeated
and her already tenuous grip on life had been further
weakened, perhaps fatally so.

She was awakened by the noise of rain dashing with un-
seasonal ferocity against the window panes on the western

side of the house. A high wind was blowing, the sea was thunderous and the roar of its full force striking the high cliffs on the western shore of the offshore islands sounded dully in the distance. Its force and fury were nevertheless unmistakable. Again and again it crashed against the rocks in an assault which seemed determined to overwhelm the islands and claim the inhabitants as its victims. The wind howled with barbaric force. Now high, now low, it was superbly orchestrated to arouse terror in all who heard it. She shuddered involuntarily and hoped that John, wherever he might be, was safely indoors. Instictively she rose and again, with a keener consciousness of physical pain than she had experienced for a long time, she inspected both doors to assure herself that they were locked. Satisfied, she returned to the fire and again fell asleep.

She was woken by a terrible pounding on the front door. A woman screamed hoarsely, "Let me in! . . . Let me in! In the name of God, let me in!" Terrorised, she remained where she was. Irrationally she thought at first it was John who was outside, despite the fact that the voice was that of a woman. Her impulse was to rush to the door and open it. She failed to move on that first impulse. The woman continued screaming and demanding admittance. Though deep and hoarse she recognised it as the voice of the young woman who had visited her earlier in the day. She knew that whatever she did, she must not admit the woman. She came trailing death. With her, she sensed, were the men who had tried to drown her by driving her out into the deep waters of the bay.

She remained, hardly breathing, by the fire. The curtains on both the front and back windows were drawn and the lamp was so low its light could hardly be seen from the outside. She heard a slight scratching and efforts were made to lift the front window. It didn't yield. Like the doors the windows had been strengthened by the former owners to protect their property against vandals during their absences for all but the summer months. She heard muttered profanities and obscenities and then the fury of the storm raged undisturbed.

She drew a deep breath and half-muttered a prayer in gratitude. Seconds later she heard the smashing of wood and glass upstairs and a raucous roar of triumph as someone gained entry into one of the rooms. She heard loud footsteps, those she assumed of a man wearing studded boots, cross to the door and try to force it. It was securely bolted top and bottom on the outside and he failed. Others entered the room. She imagined she could distinguish the soft patter of bare feet amongst all the uproar. Then they began to dance in drunken fury. They screamed in outrage and pounded the floor. She heard a man roar, "We have you now, you dirty whore of hell. We have you now, you fucking Jewish whore." The point was emphasised by everyone tramping on the bare boards of the room as though trampling something underfoot. The woman screamed, "Burn the bitch out like we did the others."

She froze, realising they might well discover her store of paraffin in the outhouse below the farmhouse. The woman screamed dementedly, "Where is he, you whore, where is me husband, Tom?"

The storm increased in force and appeared to overwhelm her. She felt herself falling into an abyss from which she believed she could never escape. She tried to scream for help but no sound issued from her mouth. The woman's words about her husband Tom rang on and on in her ears.

Daylight slanted through a slight parting in the curtains of the front window and on one elongated strip reached right across the bare boards of the floor to where she lay unconscious by the fire which had all but died out. A clot of blood showed where she glancingly struck the hearthstone when she lost consciousness. Outside the wind still howled though it had abated somewhat and the roar of the sea had lessened. Rain still dashed spasmodically against the windows. She staggered to her feet, conscious of great pain in her disjointed hip. Casually she touched the side of her head and just above the temple she located the caked blood. Had she fallen more heavily or closer to the fire, she might well have been killed. She shivered and felt intensely cold. She used the mechanical bellows to raise some life in the slumbering fire. Flames flickered into being. She fed them and in time they burned. She was about to go to the kitchen when she heard a rather furtive sound outside and then a pounding on the door. She felt herself about to lose consciousness again. A man whose voice she didn't recognise demanded entrance. He pounded on the door and eventually had the good sense to identify himself. "Open up. I'm the sergeant. . . ."

She did so. A blast of cold wind and stinging rain dashed against her as she struggled to keep the door open. A figure swathed in an oilcloth cape, a cap and leggings, slipped inside, rain streaming from his clothes. He drew off his cap and cape. To her relief she saw the dark blue uniform beneath. He was in his sixties, small but broadly built. He had silver white hair and a complexion a woman might well envy. His eyes were curiously pink. His voice was soft, whispery like that of an obsequious clergyman. He waited for some seconds until he got his breath back.

"Is your hu-," he hesitated. "Is your man in, Mam?" he asked quietly.

"No," she replied. "As a matter of fact I haven't seen him since he left for work yesterday morning. I've been expecting him all night but he hasn't returned."

He glanced sharply at her. "Did anything untoward occur last night?" His use of almost archaic English surprised her but then she thought most people in public positions do use distinct terminology.

"Yes," she said. "Some tinkers. A woman and some men broke into the back room upstairs. They tried to force the front door and then tried to raise the window, but didn't succeed. I have no idea what they wanted," she said, anticipating his next question.

"That was all that happened?"

"They spoke about burning me out . . . at least the woman did. She said. 'We'll burn her out like we did the others.'"

He drew a sharp breath and quite unconsciously whistled softly through his teeth.

"You're quite sure she said that?"

"Quite sure."

"Did you ever see the woman before?"

"Yes, she came begging yesterday. I gave her some money. She went away."

"Would you recognise her if you were to see her again?"

"Yes. I believe I would."

"Did anything else extraordinary happen?"

He sounded more like an inordinately curious male gossip than he did an interrogating policeman.

"Yes. I went for a bathe. I do so every day. Or very nearly every day."

He nodded his head in encouragement.

"Three men, tinkers I believe, stoned me. I believe they were trying to drive me out into the deeper waters where I'd drown. The currents there are very dangerous as you know."

He again nodded his silver-white head in encouragement.

"I believe . . . I firmly believe they were trying to kill me by drowning."

"And what happened . . . How did you escape? You swam to safety perhaps?"

His syrupy voice revolted her. She sensibly disguised her reaction.

"No, a man, a boy chanced along and saved me." She hesitated. "He told me his name was Petie," she said. "I asked him."

He nodded his head solemnly. "Did he now? Was that all he said?"

"Yes. I wasn't exactly at my social best. I made him go away as quickly as I could." She stared at him for some seconds. He failed to meet her eyes and turned to gaze at the fire instead and idly scratched his chin which showed some stubble. "Why are you asking me all these questions? Why have you come here?"

He remained staring at the fire as if reluctant to speak. When he did so it was with unusual deliberation.

"There was an altercation between some of the tinker men on the green above the Atlantic Hotel. Some blows were struck and then rioting broke out. What happened exactly we still don't rightly know but a can of petrol was thrown into one of the tinker's tents and a lighted match thrown in after it, setting the tent alight with fatal results for some of the occupants."

She smelt that peculiarly sweet smell of human flesh burning. She swayed until caught by a strong hand and led by a strong hand to a chair, she sat on it.

"That was stupid of me, Mam, I should have realised . . ."

"Was John involved. Did he come to any harm?"

"That I don't know. You see the man you know as John is known to others by a different name. And I daresay his real name is known only to himself. As far as I can say anything, I don't think it was —" he hesitated shortly, "John who was involved."

"Who were the victims?"

"A man, his child, both burned to death. The wife is critically ill with very little hope of recovery. They can't even shift the poor woman from the hotel."

"Don't," she shouted. "Please don't!"

He reacted rather primly, she thought.

"Of course not, Mam, but you asked and I thought it only civil . . ."

"You're quite right," she said, gaining self-control. "I did ask. It's all my fault. Are there any more questions?"

"No, Mam. Not for the present. Later perhaps I'll have to take a formal statement but for now I'd just like to inspect the place."

"Please feel free to do so."

"Thank you, Mam."

He slipped on his cape and pulled his cap over his head, snapping an elastic band under his chin. He opened the door, keeping it sufficiently apart to slip outside with great difficulty.

He had gone when she realised that he hadn't searched the house. That meant he was checking the farmhouse and outbuildings. Delight and pleasure flooded her. John could have returned last night while she was unconscious and probably thought she was sleeping when she failed to reply. He could be in the farmhouse, safe and sound. Hurriedly she dressed and slipped on her yard boots. She snatched a blanket from the bed and used it as a cloak to protect her from the rain.

Outside the force of the gale nearly swept her off her feet.
She found herself fighting for breath. There was a lamp
lighting in the farmhouse kitchen. Unmistakably it had
burned there all night. She gained the door. The sergeant
came out and caught her by the arm.

"I don't think you should go in, Mam," he shouted force-
fully.

"Why not?" she shouted in return.

He tried to restrain her. She wrenched herself free and
dashed into the kitchen.

He lay on the floor, his face bruised, his head bloodied.
A horseshoe nail transfixed his head just above the right
temple. From the small wound, a tiny, thin streak of blood
had issued and had hardened blackly. She wondered how so
small a wound could fell so big a man.

Her moaning rose steadily to a loud, protracted scream
which reverberated around the small, tidy room. Suddenly
it ceased. She was silent. She offered no resistance when
the sergeant took her by the arm and led her back to the
house.

"I'll go to town for help. I'll send out Mrs Murphy to look
after you. And make arrangements for the removal. Will you
be alright here, Mam? I have to leave you. I have no way of
getting word to the village."

She nodded her head in assurance. He stared at her un-
certainly and then deciding there was nothing further he
could do, he left.

She sat by the fireside, her hands cradled in her lap. She was
possessed of a great peace and, unaccountably, joy. She felt a
deep compassion for all those who had ever suffered in mind
or body during their travail through life on earth, or would
ever do so. She prayed for them that they might know sur-
cease — and failing that, faith, and fortitude in plenty.

She heard the sea. It was loudly mutinous, savaging the
already much-savaged shore. In its tranquil moments she
knew it to be undulous, gently murmurous and shot through

with the silver of sunlight. Its waters would grant her the oblivion she so strongly desired, an oblivion infinitely peaceful and unsurpassably fulfilling.

Rising, she went to the beach and there committed her body to the deep.

WOLFHOUND PRESS FICTION

LIAM LYNCH
Tenebrae: A Passion
Liam Lynch's second novel is a forceful, poignant record of a priest's struggle with his own inner demons. Canon Fitzgerald's loss of faith, coupled with an arrogant contempt for his parisioners and a gnawing memory of youthful thwarted affections, is precariously countered by his awareness of religious grace in a dying young woman with whom he shares a supernatural manifestation. Her death precipitates his descent into madness — the sombre *Tenebrae* of the title.

Tenebrae is the stark portrayal of the disintegration of a man who denies, and is denied love. It is a powerful and disturbing second novel from a great writer.

DOROTHY NELSON
In Night's City — a novel
'Utterly compelling . . . a magician with language and with atmosphere'

Clare Boylan, RTE Review

NIALL QUINN
Voyovic, Brigitte and Other Stories
'the whole book has the effect of astonishing originality' *John Jordan, Irish Independent*. Niall Quinn was awarded the 'Brendan Behan Memorial Fellowship for 1983.

MICHAEL MULLEN
Kelly — a novel
'certainly the funniest fantasy I have ever read' *Fantasy Today, USA*. 'Its ancestors include *The Crock of Gold*, the grotesqueries of *Finnegans Wake*, even *Jurgen*'

Punch

SAM BANEHAM
The Cloud of Desolation
'clever and imaginative essay into apocalypse fiction — an author well worth reading'

Sunday Independent

HUGH FITZGERALD RYAN
The Kybe: A novel of Ireland in Napoleonic times.